Great Timepieces

OF THE WORLD

BY CAROLINE CHILDERS
and ROBERTA NAAS

BW Publishing Associates, Inc.

IN ASSOCIATION WITH

Rizzoli International Publications, Inc.

COVER AND BACK
Patek Philippe's annual calendar, self-winding wristwatch is the first of its kind. Caliber 315 S QA automatic movement with day, date, month and sweep seconds and 24-hour indicator. Dial with luminous hands and numerals in gold. Case in 18K yellow gold.

TITLE PAGE
1912 watch by Vacheron Constantin, whose designers have revisited a Vacheron Constantin dating to the year for which it is named. Under it beats a hand-wound mechanical movement, exactly as in 1912. Individually numbered and limited to a total of 1912 models.

Minute-repeater wristwatch by Piaget. The 18K white gold case is set with 190 baguette diamonds, the center of the gold dial is adorned with eleven baguette sapphires and the small seconds indicator at nine o'clock is inlaid with mother-of-pearl.

FIRST PUBLISHED IN THE UNITED STATES OF AMERICA IN 1998 BY

Ms. Caroline Childers
and BW Publishing Associates, Inc.
11 W. 25th Street New York, NY 10010

in association with
Rizzoli International Publications, Inc.
300 Park Avenue South, New York, NY 10010

ISBN: 0-8478-2093-9
LIBRARY OF CONGRESS CATALOG CARD NUMBER: 97-076961
Disclaimer: The information contained in Great Timepieces of the World has been provided by third parties. While we believe that these sources are reliable, we assume no responsibility or liability for the accuracy of technical details contained in this book.

Every effort has been made to locate the copyright holders of materials used in this book. Should there be any errors or omissions, we apologize and shall be pleased to make acknowledgments in future editions.

Time Immemorial, Swiss Preeminence, Welcomed Complications, Chronographs, Art Deco, Enchanted Elegance, Secrets of Time, People in Time chapters written by Roberta Naas.

Logo by Danielle Loufrani

Printed in Hong Kong

CHAIRMAN
Joseph Zerbib

CHIEF EXECUTIVE OFFICER AND PUBLISHER
Caroline Childers

PRESIDENT
Yael Choukroun

EXECUTIVE PRESIDENT
Esther Tavor

EDITOR-IN-CHIEF
Natalie Warady

ART DIRECTOR
Helene Silverman

ASSISTANT TO THE PUBLISHER
Patricia Gruber

PHOTOGRAPHER
Jacques Silberstein

Contents

Robergé watches. Three models of the founding Andromède design:
Andromède RS Automatic, Andromède Regulator, Andromède RS Power Reserve.

Great Timepieces of the World

Forward

Opposite: Franck Muller
5850 RMT–Minute
Repeater Tourbillon.
A 1996 world premiere,
this mechanical watch is
manual winding with a
minute repeater striking
the hours, the quarters
and the minutes on
request. Both the
indicator of striking
mechanism and the
tourbillon are patented
by Frank Muller. Case in
950 platinum.

THAT MAN CRAFTS BY HAND MECHANISMS THAT WILL KEEP PRECISION TIME, ALL IN a space roughly the size of a quarter (and in some instances, smaller), is both overwhelming and inspiring to consider. The subject of mechanical watches is intimidating at first, with all of the intricacies of the technology, not to mention the terminology. Yet once delved into, the world of watchmaking consumes, and what quickly follows is a deep appreciation for the watchmaking skills that have been undergoing development for centuries. Perhaps more than any other profession today, the art of modern watchmaking is the summation of thousands of years worth of innovations and discovery — from the first sun-dials to Galileo to the mid-1700s, when watchmakers in Switzerland began devoting themselves to perfecting timekeeping.

Over 200 years later, that pursuit is gaining new attention. As society increasingly desires luxury goods of investment value, hand-crafted items are naturally seeing a resurgence, and in particular, mechanical watches. This is fueling the creative impulses within the great watchmaking houses, who are driven to create timepieces that once seemed impossible. For example, Patek Philippe's Caliber 89, the world's most complicated timepiece, took nine years to make before being auctioned for $3.2 million. Among its mind-numbing features is a chart displaying the celestial movements, adjustable to wherever the wearer lives. Franck Muller, a relative newcomer, is building a repertoire of patents and world premieres, including the Master Banker, his watch that features three time zones, all set with one crown.

This book is testimony to the creative energy that is emanating from Switzerland— the home of precision timing —where watchmakers are forever striving to keep pace with, and harness, time. —*Natalie Warady*

Acknowledgments

THIS BOOK COULD NOT HAVE BEEN PRODUCED WITHOUT THE ASSISTANCE AND KINDNESS OF MANY PEOPLE who generously shared with us their knowledge and experience of the watchmaking industry. We want to thank Mr. Peter Laetsch, president of the Federation of the Swiss Watchmaking Industry in the United States and his wife Sylvia, for their enduring friendship and support. We want to express our gratitude to all individuals and companies who devoted their time and patience: Mr. Jean-Claude Biver, Mr. Ricardo Guadalupe from Blancpain, Switzerland; Ms. Béatrice Vuille, Ms. Sonia Battaglia from Breguet, Switzerland; Ms. Valerie Burgat from Breitling, Switzerland, Ms. Anne Walle from Breitling, USA; Ms. Julie Keating from Cartier, USA; Mr. Pierre Haquet, Ms. Evelyne Ménager from Chaumet, Paris, Mr. Daniel Bogue from Chaumet, USA; Ms. Caroline Gruosi-Scheufele, Ms. Annick Benoit-Godet from Chopard, Switzerland. Mr. William Furhmann from Chopard, USA; Ms. Jeanne Massaro, Ms. Diana Moran, Mr. Harry Viola, Ms. Livia Marotta, Mr. John Rooney from Concord; Mr. Hratch Kaprielian, Ms. Katie Kinsella from Franck Muller, USA, Ms. Cristina D'Agostino From Franck Muller, Switzerland; Mr. Luigi Macaluso, Ms. Sylvie Rumo, Jacqueline Briggen from Girard Perregaux, Switzerland, Mr. Ron Jackson from Girard Perregaux, USA; Ms. Vanessa Neuenhaus from Harry Winston; Mr. Henry-John Belmont, Ms. Corine Paget-Blanc, Ms. Elisabeth Schnebelen, Ms. Valérie Tacconi from Jaeger-LeCoultre, Switzerland, Ms. Laura Jo-Boynton, Ms. Nancy Fox from Jaeger-LeCoultre, USA; Mr. Alex Kull, Mr. Venanzio Ciampa from Omega, Switzerland, Ms. Béatrice de Quervan from Omega, USA; Mr. Erik Dochtermann, Ms. Jennifer Jones from K.D. & E.; Mr. Hugues-Olivier Borès, Mrs. Pamela G. Cloutier from Patek Philippe, Switzerland; Mr. Yves Piaget, Mr. Francis Gouten, Mr. Charris Yadigaroglou from Piaget, Switzerland; Mr. Alain Jeker, Ms. Stéphanie Berger from Robergé, Switzerland; Mr. Herman Plotnik, Ms. Michelle Di Leo from Vacheron Constantin, USA; Mr. Claude D. Proellochs, Mr. Patrick Ketterer from Vacheron Constantin Switzerland; Mr. Jean Weber, Ms. Catherine Brandt from Van Cleef & Arpels, Switzerland, Mr. Jacques Arpels, Mr. Eric Arpels, Mr. Ferdinand Ripoll, Ms. Marie Moatti-Beauchard, from Van Cleef & Arpels, Paris, Mr. Henri Barguirdjian, Mr. Guy Bedarida, Ms. Paula Peterson, Mr. Claude Arpels from Van Cleef & Arpels, New York. We also want to thank those who provided a wealth of information to complete this book: Mr. Jean Siegenthaler from Editions Scriptar S.A., for use of the book Watchmaking and History, Art, Science, by Catherine Cardinal, Masterpieces of Watchmaking, by Luigi Pippa. We would also like to give a special thanks to Frenchway Travel, who make the impossible mission, possible. Finally, our most heartfelt thanks is extended to Mr. Joseph Zerbib, a tireless source of strength who supported us every step of the way and without whom Great Timepieces of the World would not be possible. —*Caroline Childers*

Opposite:Chopard men's watch housing the new LUC movement, named in tribute to the watchmaker's founder, Louise Ulysse Chopard. In 18K yellow gold with white dial and gold hour markers.

to my mother

The Essence of Time

When I was first approached about writing this book, I was filled with trepidation. I love the watch industry. I've been a journalist reporting about it for nearly 15 years; it's as though watches are in my blood. Still, the thought of tying together the historical elements involved, profiling the different eras in watchmaking and chronicling different types of watches immediately evoked in me a multitude of concerns. But, as I embarked on my research and investigations, I became even more enthralled with the concept not only of watchmaking, but of time itself.

One glimpse back to the dawn of man and we immediately grasp the longevity of time. To the living, time is immediate: it is minutes, hours, days, perhaps even weeks, or years, but the inimitable nature of this constantly moving "thing" nearly eliminates the concept of the present. And, by so doing, it forces us into the hopeless corner of trying to harness it in our insatiable desire to track and conquer time. But, while this elusive "thing" maintains its mystifying hold over us, thanks to man's unyielding curiosity and painstaking quest we can, at least, measure time — not only effectively, but elegantly.

The significance of time in our lives can perhaps best be exemplified by the multitude of clocks in the workplace, clocks in recreational areas, clocks on computers and watches on the wrist. It is estimated that the average individual owns at least four watches — a number that is on the rise.

Interestingly, the popularity of watches today stems from a recently recognized polarity: watches are no longer just instruments to measure time. They are fashion and lifestyle statements: items of pride. For many, the timepiece worn on the wrist offers a tiny glimpse into the personality of the wearer. This may be why so many collectors, connoisseurs and watch enthusiasts turn to fine Swiss watches as the object of choice, for it is from this tiny country that the world's most innovative and luxurious timepieces emerge.

continued on page 13

The music of time plays beautifully on this Minute Repeater from Blancpain. Unchallenged as a supreme watchmaking feat, the minute repeater is the only watch that truly "tells" time. It took Blancpain's master watchmakers more than 10,000 hours to develop and fine-tune this minute repeater. Only five or six leave the Blancpain workshop each month. It chimes the hours, quarter-hours and minutes, each with its own distinctive sound and frequency.

Generations of families spanning centuries have embraced the fine art of Swiss watchmaking. Mastering the horological trade with an eagerness and enthusiasm that yields some of the finest masterpieces in history, Switzerland's watchmakers are unrivaled.

A visit to the workshops of high-end watch producers is much like a trip through time, history and culture. In some of the world's most elite and prestigious watch factories lies a marvel of heritage and craftsmanship that is both unparalleled and, to some degree, unbelievable. Many of these watch producers still employ old watchmaking techniques. Master craftsmen spend hours at tables hand-carving movements, setting stones, finishing pieces — in short achieving a perfect blend of modern technology and ancient craft.

I have visited dozens of watch factories over the years and each time I walk through the quiet, almost hallowed halls and work areas, I am profoundly impressed. The minute and intricate work is a marvel to me and I often find myself wondering what makes the people behind the watches tick. Whatever it is, it's powerful. Watchmakers persist in their untiring efforts to invent new watchmaking techniques, new timekeeping functions and additional complicated movements.

It is this dedication, along with the allure of their work — the craftsmanship, precision and art — that makes the finest Swiss watches reign supreme. And wearing a timepiece borne of this intensity is perhaps as close as one can come to mastering time.

The timepieces portrayed herein offer an insight into the technical prowess and genius behind a single item that transcends languages and borders. The pages of this book pay homage to some of the finest watchmaking houses in the world, to the heritage and footsteps they continue in, and the legacies they give to us to leave to our grandchildren: Great Timepieces of the World.

Roberta Naas

Roberta Naas

In a 25th anniversary celebration, Omega introduced this commemorative platinum, skeleton Speedmaster in a limited series of 50 pieces, each individually numbered and engraved. The satin-finished case sides also has engraved "Apollo XI 1969-1994". This wonderful timepiece features gold hour markers, sapphire case back to reveal the hand-finished mechanical chronograph movement, and a platinum bracelet.

Time Immemorial

SINCE THE DAWN of man, the sun has rose and set, the tides have changed and "time" has passed by swiftly. So swiftly, in fact, that man has spent centuries desperately trying to capture time, keep time, or at the very least, measure time — probably in the futile hopes of harnessing it. Time eludes and overpowers man. This abstract, illusive "thing" of moving seconds, minutes, hours, days and years is often incomprehensible, primarily because it has no physical being. Time cannot be seen or touched — its fleeting nature makes its measurement challenging. True enough, today we understand the concept of time and we have advanced technologically to be able to measure time to the tiniest fraction of a second; but still we are restrained by its sweeping progress and its authoritarian hold on our lives. Time was perhaps even more perplexing and mystifying centuries ago, when man had only the sun and moon to track time.

Until the advent of clocks and watches as we know them today, the measurement of time throughout the centuries underwent elaborate changes. Because the attempts to measure time span more than 20 centuries, it stands to reason that there are many theories regarding time measurement methods, dates and even inventors.

Initially, most time keeping methods were closely intertwined with the elements of the universe — the moon, sun, stars. It is generally argued that astronomy was the guiding force behind such monumental structures as Stonehenge, or several pre-Colombian temples. Indeed, most ancient civilizations relied solely on the movement of celestial bodies to determine planting seasons, harvest times, or some special day or time of significance to their religious beliefs.

For the primitive man, days began at sunrise and went until sunset; nights lasted from sunset to sunrise. And because at that time man's only real needs were to hunt, plant or harvest in order to stay alive, calendars were sufficient. However, as time passed, and life became slightly more complex, man wished to measure more immediate time segments. And as centuries trekked by and man became even more self sufficient, more succinct timekeeping methods became imperative.

Of course a majority of time needs in the first dozen centuries or so of timekeeping were dictated by monastic rules. Prayer was important in every culture, and often people broke their days into various worship constraints and times.

Primitive Time Tracking

The most primitive method of measuring time was tracking shadows. Probably not long after the dawn of man, humans began measuring shadows as they fell across one's

body. Old references indicate measurement of time by the shadow of one's foot, or entire body.

From there, man attempted to measure time with a vertical rod or upright stick in the ground surrounded by rocks. As the sun moved, the shadow grew and reached the rocks at different times — thereby allowing more precise segmented measurement. These sticks and stones from 3,000 BC, in their crudest form, are the forefather of what was to become the sundial — an instrument that measures time based on the shadow of a pointer cast by the sun onto a dial.

The Chinese and the Egyptians each had their own version of the sundial as early as 1500 BC. Sundials were one of the most agreeable methods of timekeeping developed. They indicated temporal hours based on geographic latitude. To tell time accurately for the location one is in, the dial must be adjusted to the proper latitude and the angle of the pointer (off of which the shadow is cast) must face due north. As a result of their ease of construction, a great variety of sundials developed over the centuries and across the continents.

The most monumental sundial type structures include Stonehenge (presumably built around 2000 BC) and the Egyptian obelisks. Often more than a hundred feet high, obelisks were symbols of the sun god Ra in Egyptian culture. It is believed that the earliest known obelisk was built around 2000 BC. Egyptian priests referred to the obelisk as the "finger of God;" the Greeks referred to it as a gnomon (one who knows).

Perhaps the greatest drawback to the sundial was, and remains today, the fact that the sun is not always shining. Thus, more efficient instruments to measure time were sought. Around the same time, some cultures were utilizing timekeeping methods that involved the burning of such things as oil, candles and even incense. Time was measured based on how fast the substance burned away. (Although candles were used early on in history, it was not until the second half of the 9th century that the English king, Alfred of the Western Saxons, invented the

Above: It is believed that the earliest obelisks date back to 2000 BC. Egyptians measured time based on the shadows of the obelisk.

Above right: Combining two needs in one item, this unusual piece, circa 1590, is a gun powder flack with a built-in sundial.

Below: Sundials represented the most widely used method of telling time both before and after the inception of the water clock. This sundial, circa 1599, is crafted in ivory.

Background: Sometimes, the Egyptians built steps on the pyramids and determined the time based on where the shadows fell across the steps.

candle clock.) Another substance sometimes used to measure time was sand. In fact, while sand was probably first used about 350 BC, it was used centuries later (beginning in the early 1300s) in the hourglass.

Making their general appearance somewhat later than sundials, in 325 BC, were clepsydras, or water clocks. The Greeks are generally credited with developing the first clepsydra — which measures time with water. The clepsydra ("water thief") was an ingenious device that developed into many variations on its original principal. With this device water flowed from one container to another at a steady rate. There were markings on the containers so that the Greeks could measure the passage of time by the water level. Other societies measured the passage of time based on the outflow of a certain amount of water though a hole or sieve. In Greece and Rome clepsydras were used to limit the amount of time lawyers, judges and politicians could make speeches.

Water clocks remained integral timekeeping and measuring

formats for many cultures and many centuries. It was not until later—probably around the year 900 AD — that they were equipped with mechanisms that moved to strike the hours. In fact, in 1090 Su Song presented what is believed to be China's first water clock to the emperor. The movements of a tower clock, which was 30-feet high, were driven by water from buckets. The clock had bells that rang every 15 minutes.

However, just as sundials were reliant upon the sun shining to accurately tell time, water clocks were also dependent upon the elements. In the dead of winter, most water clocks flowed more slowly and eventually froze over. Other problems with water clocks arose during drought, or extreme heat where evaporation was an issue.

Eventually scientists realized they needed to rely on some other driving power. With this in mind, they set forth on a new embarkment — the concept of measuring time with clocks driven by weights moving up and down. The problem with this idea, however, came with the challenge of making the weights rise and fall uniformly and regularly so that time did not go astray.

In an effort to find a solution to this problem, the foliot was invented. Essentially the foliot is a cross-bar (balance) and two

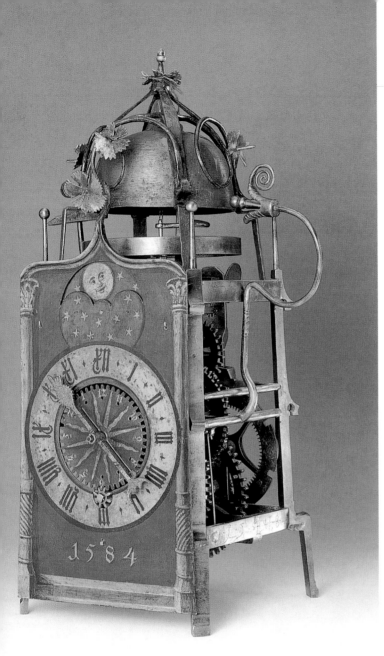

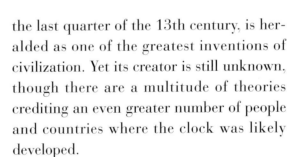

the last quarter of the 13th century, is heralded as one of the greatest inventions of civilization. Yet its creator is still unknown, though there are a multitude of theories crediting an even greater number of people and countries where the clock was likely developed.

Medieval monks, required to pray at precise moments of the day were driven by a desire to measure time correctly. They wanted a clock that would ring a bell at regular intervals. However, despite this drive, and despite the fact that the mechanical clock made its first appearance on the scene in the 13th century, it did not take its rightful place in history until the 14th century.

Medieval Mechanics

Interestingly, the first mechanical clocks were made primarily by blacksmiths and gun founders, as they were the most adept at

weights (regulators), one at each end of the horizontal cross bar. The bar is fixed to a vertical rod (verge) on which there are two pallets. It is these pallets that engage in a toothed wheel and push the vertical rod back and forth, there by causing the foliot to oscillate. The device that regulates power in a mechanical clock, even today, is known as the escapement.

The invention of the escapement, foliot and verge, naturally gave birth to the mechanical clock. Its invention, traced to

Right: Created around the year 1600, this ivory portable sundial is decorated with garnets and emeralds.

Bottom center: This style of watch, called the Nuremberg Egg because of its shape and origin, was one of the earliest watches worn. This particular timepiece was created around 1550. Its case is of gilt-copper and the back cover bears a bell for the striking mechanism. The oval movement is made completely of iron.

Below: Renaissance neck watch in oval format, circa 1590, features an alarm. The watch has a small horizontal sundial and is created in gold.

working with iron. Typically these clocks consisted of a weight, an energy-driving mechanism, an escapement and a striking or pointing element. It is believed that the clocks, while accurate for their time, lost about 15 minutes per day in their timekeeping.

So with the dawn of the 14th century, mechanical monumental clocks started to appear — albeit, slowly. There are still either records or actual monumental clocks in existence testifying to this. It is generally believed that prior to 1350, there were only three public mechanical clocks — all in Italy. There was a clock in existence in 1335 in Milan that offered a large clapper that struck a bell to indicate the hours of the day and night. Another such masterpiece is the astronomical clock created in 1344 by Jacopo di Dondi for the entrance tower of the palace at Padua.

It was during the 14th century that the hand bells evolved into a mechanical method of a train of wheels causing a hammer to strike the bells — the crude forerunner of what we today call repeaters. The first mechanical striking clock did not appear until about 1370 in France (though England also lays claim to a monument clock with bells in this year). The clock in France was built in the square tower of the Palais de Justice in Paris and was built by Henri le Vic.

During this time, blacksmiths began making clocks in what they thought to be more manageable sizes, but these were large and heavy. Generally the clocks were hung in the hallways of large homes and its bells were loud enough to be heard in every room of the house. Astronomical clocks, too, began gaining in importance in both England and France.

In the 15th century, as the Middle Ages gave way to the Renaissance, a wealth of cultural developments hurled the world into a new age of art, literature, science, philosophy, religion and beauty. With this came a renewed interest in objects of art, and so a great focus was placed on the development of "table" clocks. This development led to a grand variety of smaller portable clocks in history.

In the 16th century with the rise of the High Renaissance came experimentation into new metals for clocks. No longer was iron the only metal of choice. In fact, it was at this point in time that brass, bronze and even silver began being utilized in clock

making. Also during the 16th century, springs entered the world of clock making to replace weights. It was Peter Henlein of Nuremberg, Germany — one of the famous clock making centers of the time — who, in the first decade of the 1500s made two important contributions to the world of clock and watchmaking. He was the first to offer a small clock movement in an elongated case — thereby creating the first watch. Because of its shape, it and subsequent pieces, became known as the Nuremberg eggs. More importantly, however, he executed the idea of a spring driven clock. This clock worked for 40 hours before it needed to be wound and it chimed the hours. Thus, Henlein is credited with producing the first clock driven by what we today call a mainspring.

Some experts believe that Henlein's

Left and above: Interior and exterior of enamel timepiece from the 17th century. Enamel work became an important decorative function of watches and clocks.

Bottom: By the 17th century, clock design and materials became advanced. This Renaissance table clock, circa 1640, is crafted of a bronze lion and small dog. The clock dial is sliver with enamel design, the base is wood. As the clock works, both the lion and the dog move their eyes to keep time with the clock. As the hour strikes, the lion opens its mouth and moves its wings.

Above: This watch, dating to the beginning of the 17th century, is crafted in silver and brass in the oval format typical of the era.

Below: Leonardo da Vinci was obsessed with the precise measurement of time.

Bottom right: It was only in 1995 that it was found that a drawing of Leonard da Vinci's, thought to be a motor or a flying machine, turned out to be a workable spring driven clock movement.

16th century invention was probably based on the pictures and notes of the 15th century scientist, inventor and artist Leonardo da Vinci. In fact, a close look at the works and genius of Leonardo indicate that he may have been the inventor of this device. Obsessed with timekeeping and time measurement, Leonardo devoted a great deal of his life to the subject.

A fanatic about precise timekeeping, Leonardo was fascinated with the advent of the mechanical clock, which had changed society's path from the Middle Ages. Leonardo traveled and sketched countless clocks and their escapements in his notebooks. It was in these notebooks that he meticulously sketched gear trains, and described an appliance for the manufacture of springs and mechanisms. He even attempted — on paper — to devise a single-wheel clock. Nevertheless, Henlein retains credit for creating the first mainspring clock.

The middle of the 16th century ushered in several other changes throughout Europe with respect to clock making. In 1541 when he banned people from wearing jewelry, Reformist John Calvin unknowingly altered Switzerland's future. Geneva's jewelers, goldsmiths and engravers were forced by Calvin's mandate to learn another craft. Refugees from France and Italy

taught them the art of watchmaking. It was three years later, in 1544, that King Francois 1 of France legitimized the clock making industry by creating the first known guild of clock makers.

A quarter of a century later, pocket watches made their appearance. In fact, the oldest known pocket watch dates back to 1574. While the watchmaker is unknown, it is a superb piece of craftsmanship. Made of bronze, the watch pictures Saint George slaying a dragon. It is framed in a laurel wreath and the back of the watch depicts the Crucifixion.

Further advances in timekeeping came in the 17th century with the advent of the pendulum clock. Until this point, as stated earlier, most mechanical clocks lost approximately 15 minutes a day. But the

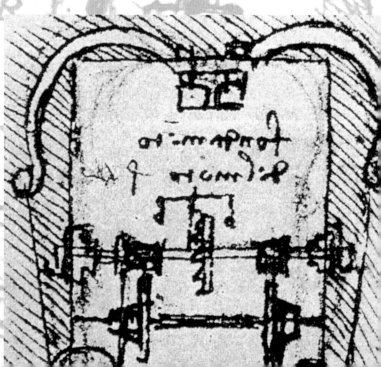

pendulum clock brought about the most precise timekeeping to date. The story of the pendulum is generally believed to have begun with Galileo in 1583 when in his cathedral in Pisa he watched a lamp swing back and forth with incredible regularity. Using his pulse to time the intervals he deduced that the periods of swing were all of equal time. He investigated these principals and years later suggested the development of an accurate timepieces using a pendulum.

It was, in fact, a Dutch scientist in the 17th century named Christian Huygens who, in 1656, patented a pendulum clock he had designed. This design — the intended use of which was for ships at sea — was for a miniature clock. Although the clock failed its test on the high seas, it proved to be an integral contribution to timekeeping. With the accuracy of these clocks came a great move toward pendulums in most clocks. In 1680, with accuracy down pat, the first minute hands were added to clocks. Ten years later, in 1690, the second hand made its appearance.

As the 17th century progressed, timekeeping reached new technological heights. Until this time the key clock and watch industry was dominated by the English and Germans, who needed precise equipment for their naval forces. But the tides were about to change.

Clock makers scaled down and began creating smaller, portable clocks for travel, and at the same time, watches became canvases for artistic beauty. Clocks were often engraved and adorned with stones, and the influence of nature inspired the depictions of flowers and scenery on timepieces. Watch faces themselves were being adorned with precious stones, while the cases were painted with enamel designs.

Improvements in movements yielded smaller and smaller workings. Table clocks had long since developed into traveling clocks complete with compass, and into portable clocks that were hung on the belt (the forerunners of watches), then into pocket watches and, finally, of course, the emergence of the wristwatch. In the 18th century, watchmakers in Switzerland had attained optimum skills in crafting watch movements, enabling the country to assume a leading role where the rest of the world had left off.

Swiss Preeminence

THE RISE OF SWITZERLAND as the epitome of fine watchmaking was centuries in the making. Today the country is renown for its technical prowess in the creation of some of the world's most complicated and wonderful watches. A multitude of factors came into play to promote the art of watchmaking in general and to lay the foundation for the rise of Switzerland as the premiere watchmaking center of the world — a title the tiny country indisputably holds to this day. Perhaps the earliest driving force propelling Switzerland to its eventual role was an act promulgated centuries ago. In 1541, when the stern Protestant reformist John Calvin banned the wearing of jewelry, Geneva's jewelers, goldsmiths and engravers — faced with destitution — were forced to seek other lines of work. At the same time, Geneva became a haven for French and other refugees who brought with them the knowledge and skills of watchmaking. In no time, Geneva's artisans mastered the intricate craft of making precision timepieces.

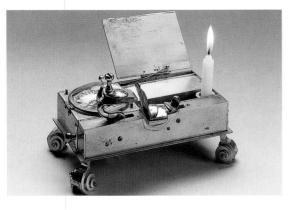

Above: In the late 18th century, clocks were appearing in all forms, especially combined with other utilitarian functions. This clock, circa 1770, is combined with a Flintlock Alarm. Giltcase on four rolled feet, with a silver Champléve dial featuring a central alarm plate with two winding stems. A lever on the right of the case opens the case top allowing the flintlock mechanism to generate a spark that ignites the candle, which was also raised when the lever was pushed. The lighting is achieved by a mechanism that is triggered by the alarm (which also sets off an acoustical bell). The alarm is set by filling a small channel with gunpowder.

Right: The elegant styling of the mid-18th century is reflected in this clock created by Pierre Jaquet-Droz. It has a chime and a set of flutes to play six melodies. It features a pendulum movement, verge escapement and locking plate.

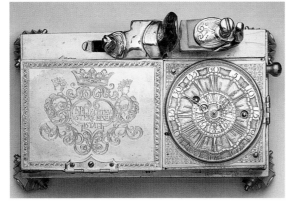

As Calvin believed the watch to be a necessary item rather than a piece of jewelry, watchmaking was acceptable — and jewelers, enamelers and similar artisans joined forces with watchmakers, clock makers and cabinotiers. This melding of great trades, talents and minds gave rise to the first true creation of fine Swiss watches. Thus, it was in the 16th century that Switzerland — and Geneva in particular — made its foray into the clock and watch arena. The city became a creative center and new influences arose, yielding new heights of aesthetic beauty and technical prowess.

In 1601, Geneva's watchmakers organized to regulate their profession and formed the first Watchmakers' Guild of Geneva — with 500 members. By the beginning of the 18th century, as these 500 master watchmakers employing at least 1,000 apprentices began moving about Switzerland, watchmaking proliferated. Watchmakers settled their practices and workshops in outlying areas such has Neuchatel, Basel and the Jura mountains. Conditions were ripe for the expansion and maturation of the Swiss watch industry.

The 18th Century

With clocks a "staple" of most homes of the wealthy, and watches assuming a similar must-have status, the 18th century was burgeoning with growth, excitement and advancements. A great majority of the clocks from the first half of the 18th century represent Baroque styling — reminiscent of the period of Louis XIV. However, clock designs knew no middle ground; if they were not ornate, they were contrastingly simple. Because clocks were subject to problems if they encountered too much dust or dirt, clock mechanisms became totally enclosed. By the early 1700s, wood had become the predominant material of choice and painted wooden clocks became prevalent.

Design flourished as engraved copper and gold applications, as well as enamel and inlaid arts (including tortoise shell, mother of pearl and later mosaic), took on new decorative meaning. Similarly, engrav-

ing became an important design motif. Flora and fauna were initially the most popular themes, but themes of love, beauty and eroticism soon surfaced, as did watches depicting the Madonna and other religious themes. Mythological, historical or biblical images were revered. Of similar importance were coats of arms, heraldic art and, finally, intimately personal scenes of valor, honor and love.

Aside from design advances evident in the 18th century, clock makers continued focusing on creating and perfecting a variety of different escapements and other innovations. There was new determination to create smaller and flatter watches, to develop even more precise methods of timekeeping and to scintillate with surprise and invention.

During this century, came the development of several important escapements used in clocks, including the dead beat escapement devised by England's George Graham in 1715 (which a slight push to the pendulum in such away that it offers less interference to the movement thereby offering greater precision), his cylinder escapement (which was more accurate than a crown wheel on the verge escapement), and the detached Lever escapement (which uses a lever to activate the balance wheel), created by Thomas Mudge in 1759.

Yet as each phase seemed to reach a pinnacle, the quest was on to be better, different, more exciting. It was this yearning for perfection in Swiss watchmaking that finally led to the establishment of some of the world's greatest watchmaking houses in Switzerland.

Left: As the 18th century led into the 19th century, watchmaking emerged in smaller, more gracious formats. The top pair of watches here, circa 1795, were made by William Anthony of London for the Chinese market. They feature gold and blue enamel set with pearls and diamonds. The center watch is a finely enameled snuff box with built-in watch. The two bottom watches are both from the house of Breguet. The one on the left, circa 1810, is called the "kitchen" and features an automaton scene; the one on the right is a gold quarter repeating half-skeleton wandering hour watch.

Center: Snuff box with watch and automaton is finely engraved and all sides are blue enameled, circa 1790. The top consists of three lids that open individually. The watch is in the compartment on the right, the middle is the snuff box, and the left compartment contains the automaton scene "Cupid's smithy" that starts moving when the cover is lifted. The automaton is an angel that operates a pair of bellows at the forge with a glowing fire. the second Cupid forges the love arrows with a sledge hammer while a windmill turns in the background.

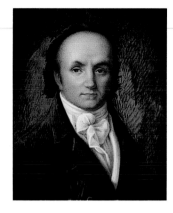

Top: Abraham-Louis Breguet, considered the father of watchmaking.

Above: Gold, self-winding "Perpetuelle" pocket watch (no. 5) from Breguet featuring a quarter repeating movement with phases and age of the moon and winding indicator.

Center: Breguet, in 1793, created the "Pendule Sympathique." Heralded in history for its ingenuity, the company still produces a very limited number of this clock today, most of which retail for about $1 million. The watch is automatically set and wound daily when placed into the recess at the top of the clock. This particular set features a hand-wound open-worked skeleton watch with tourbillon, compensating balance spring with Breguet overcoil.

Right: From Breguet's archives is the register entry that attests to the sale of a repeater wristwatch to the Queen of Naples recorded on December 5, 1811.

Among the first on the scene: Jean-Marc Vacheron, who, at the age of 24 was accepted as a master watchmaker. In 1755 he established the firm that today is known as Vacheron Constantin — the oldest watch company in the world. Nearly two and a half centuries old, this venerable house has created some of the most spectacular timepieces in history and today.

In the realm of technical prowess, advancements were ceaseless. In 1770, Abraham Louis Perrelet invented a winding mechanism that operated in both directions via a rotor. It is considered the forerunner of the automatic watch and was later improved upon by Abraham-Louis Breguet in France, making possible the perpetual movement. Also in 1770, Jean Antoine Lepine created a type of movement that satisfied the demands of the day for a flatter watch that could be carried in "fob" pockets to conceal them from potential thieves. The Lepine caliber was adopted by many watch companies and is still in use today.

With such a futuristic spirit pulsating during the second half of the 18th century, watchmakers forged ahead, eventual-ly dispensing with large, bulky movements and turning to clean, elegant design.

While the creative development was pervasive within the watchmaking community, Breguet is generally credited as the forefather of modern watchmaking. Born in 1747, in Neuchatel, the young Breguet moved to Paris when he was 15 years old and it was there that he acquired much of his theoretical and practical training. He opened Montres Breguet, in 1775. His career was marked by invention, innovation and distinction. Breguet was greatly admired by King Louis XVI and Queen Marie Antoinette, as well as Napoleon I, and was considered the watchmaker of choice for them, and later for the Tsar of Russia, the Sultan of the

Ottoman Empire, and the Queen of Naples.

In 1780, he created the first in a series of masterful triumphs: the development of what he termed the Perpetuelle watch, the first automatic self-winding watch built on principals first introduced by Perrelet. Later, in 1789, he invented an oil-free escapement and a winding key, which later became known as the "drunkard's key" because it prevented accidental time changes due to careless handling. Among Breguet's other inventions: the constant force escapement, the overcoil balance spring and the first modern carriage clock, which was sold to Napoleon Bonaparte.

Breguet also is credited with other important inventions: the gong spring, which considerably reduced the width of repeater watches; the fall-breaking safety device, the first shock-resistant system; the perpetual calendar watch that automatically takes into account the leap year.

It is generally believed that just about the turn of the century, in 1790, the earliest known wristwatch appeared. It is credited to Jacquet-Droz

and Paul Leschot of Geneva, Switzerland. As the century progressed, so did the reputation of Switzerland as an important player in watchmaking. While the Swiss expertise rested, it seems, in the creation of complicated timepieces, Geneva was the leading producer of watches by the end of the 18th century.

The 19th Century

With the turn of the century, Swiss watchmakers made several astute changes in production that would cement their future as the preeminent leaders in watchmaking. They opted against the verge escapement and instead began using the Lepine caliber and cylinder escapement. Of equal importance, Swiss watchmakers were receptive to mass production.

At the same time, their counterparts in England were reluctant to embrace the new technology, even though they held the prime seat of production for the highly precise chronometer. With their continual refusal to abandon the fusee and verge escapement for the cylindri-

Above: In 1770, Abraham Louis Perrelet created a double-direction winding mechanism that constituted the first automatic watch.

Top row and bottom center: The art of decoration was significant in the 19th century, especially as jewels were used. This masterpiece by Patek Philippe, circa 1846, is encrusted with diamonds and rubies. The photo far left reveals the case back of the watch, revealing the movement, the photo next to it reveals the inside of the pocket watch, featuring an elegant ruby-red enameled dial.

Above: As the 19th century progressed, emphasis was placed on development. Until about 1820, watches were wound and set with a key, as with this elegant watch by Girard-Perregaux that was lodged inside a specially made Florentine double-ducat holder.

Below: In 1878, Ami LeCoultre created what was great masterpiece of its time. This watch was exhibited at the International Universal Exhibition in Paris in 1878 and won a bronze medal. It features many complications, including a perpetual calendar, hours and minutes indicator, an hour circle for the alarm, phases and age of the moon, month and days of the week indicator, power reserve, repeater mechanism and a thermometer.

cal escapement, they lost their foothold in the market. Eventually, the English watchmaking tradition would completely fall.

In 1810, Breguet created one of the first known wristwatch for the Queen of Naples. In documentation only recently uncovered in the archives of Breguet, on folio 29, it is found that on June 8, 1810, the Queen of Naples (Caroline Murat) the younger sister of Emperor Napoleon the 1st, placed an order with Breguet for two watches: one, order number 2639 of the Breguet production, designated as a "repeater watch in oblong shape for wristlet."

While wristwatches appeared intermittently through the 1800s, they remained a novelty until somewhere around 1880, when they started appearing on the wrists of women. During the interim eight decades, leaps in progress were realized.

Around 1820 the keyless clock emerged. Until this point, with just a few exceptions, clocks were wound and set with a key. The focus over the next few decades centered on the development of a winding system for setting clocks and watches. In 1820, Thomas Prest, an English watchmaker, had taken out a patent for a pendant winding mechanism. Because he had abandoned the winding key, he proposed setting the hands of the clock with one's finger.

In 1822, Nicolas Rieussec took out a five-year patent for a "timekeeper or device to measure the distance traveled, called seconds chronograph" — paving the way for hundreds of years of research into this specialty that today enjoys its own prestige in the world of timekeeping. In 1830, Breguet introduced watches with a button for setting the time.

In 1833, Charles-Antoine LeCoultre, one of a long line of LeCoultres, opened his workshop in the Vallée de Joux. He immediately set to work creating masterpieces and making developments in movements. By 1860, LeCoultre employed 100 people and

became an early source for complicated movements, particularly repeaters and calendars.

In 1835, Louis Audemars, a founding father of Audemars Piguet, sold watches with a pendant winding mechanism that both wound the spring and set the hands. In 1842, Adrien Philippe exhibited a pendant winding watch at the Paris Exhibition that consisted of a double system of winding the watch. He won a gold medal for this and, more importantly, attracted the attention of Antoine Norbert de Patek, who had founded his own watch company in 1939. Later the two joined forces to establish the Patek Philippe watch company.

In 1845, Philippe was issued a patent for his winding mechanism — a device that set the hands by pulling out the winding button. Two years later, in 1847, Charles Antoine LeCoultre introduced winding button mechanisms that set the hands with a side button. It was the LeCoultre and Philippe principles that were most widely used thereafter, and it is primarily Philippe's principle that is used in watches today.

It was during the later half of this century that the era of complicated watches was cemented in Swiss history. With the best minds working tirelessly at developing timekeeping methods, innovations poured forth and timepieces included such specialized features as the perpetual calendar, minute chimes, alarms, tide tables, independent seconds hands, multiple dial chronographs and the fly-back hand (for recording multiple finishing times during races). By the last quarter of the century, watches seemed to have every possible measurement feature available — tachometric scales for transport emerged, astronomical

Top center: Chopard's first pocket watch was created in 1860. Crafted in silver, it housed Chopard's first complicated movement.

Above: As goldsmithing became increasingly ornamental, arabesque-patterned cases became ubiquitous. Vacheron Constantin's 1841 pendant watch for women features an elegantly enameled case front and back.

Left: Omega has the distinction of introducing what may be the world's first minute-repeater wristwatch. Created by Louis Brandt in 1892, the watch features a striking mechanism that chimes, on demand, the hours, quarter hours and minutes.

Above: In 1904 aviator Santos-Dumont ordered a wristwatch from Cartier and the special-order item became a staple in the Cartier collection about a decade later. This Santos timepiece was made in 1928.

Bottom right: Alberto Santos Dumont and his flying machine.

Below: Jaeger-LeCoultre is credited with creating the first reversible wristwatch, the Reverso, as well as the world's smallest mechanical movement, caliber 101.

measurements made their appearances, as did thermometers, altimeters and even slide rules.

The next step was to perfect automation. While it had been earlier, in 1839, that Auguste Leschot had introduced the first machines capable of manufacturing what were considered interchangeable watch parts, the concept had not yet been fully embraced.

With the rise of the industrial revolution, "mass" production came into play and truly influenced the watchmaking trade. Further mechanization of watchmaking was inevitable and eventually the full-fledged implementation of certain machine-made parts brought Switzerland full-scale prominence and glory in the world of watchmaking.

statement and a new jewelry adornment, caught flak from men who believed women had no business wearing watches.

Meanwhile, soldiers in the Prussian war found wristwatches more convenient and thought of them as part of their uniform. In 1904, aviator Santos-Dumont ordered a wristwatch from Cartier so that he could read the time on his wrist without having to release the controls of this plane. Gradually, those whose livelihood's demanded precision timing began examining the concept of a wristwatch.

It was the outbreak of the first World War in 1914 that changed the future of the wristwatch. Suddenly aviators and artillery officers realized the efficiency of watches on the wrist and orders poured into factories. By the end of World War I, the fate of wristwatches as an acceptable, even

The 20th Century

While watches on the wrist had made token appearances throughout several centuries, it was not until the 20th century that wristwatches truly emerged in full swing. Initially, the wearing of a watch on a wrist was met with consternation and, to some degree, hostility. Women, who thought wristwatches to be a fashion

preferable, form of telling time was sealed.

Even though the watch was firmly out of the pocket, it was far from perfect. Wristwatches were oversized and bulky, and craftsmen dedicated themselves to scaling down the interior mechanisms so that wristwatches could be smaller and more attractive.

Piaget produced a miniature minute repeater movement, though it did not commercially use this movement in watches for nearly 50 years. Around 1915 Vacheron Constantin manufactured a small baguette movement, and in 1929, LeCoultre launched the caliber 101 — which still holds the record in the Guinness Book of World Records for being the smallest mechanical watch movement.

Timing became important in this era in new terms. In fact, Breitling Watch Company is credited with patenting and marketing the first stopwatch with a 30-minute

indicator and a center sweephand. Called the Vitesse (speed), the watch was in popular demand by police officers who used it to check road traffic speeds. Breitling took the stopwatch concept several steps further by putting it into wristwatch format, creating the Vitesse and Montbrillant lines.

In the 1920s, wristwatches made their foray in to the world of private aviation, and in 1927, after his solo flight across the Atlantic, Charles Lindbergh invented the Hour-Angle watch, sending the original design to Longines for development. Also in the 20s a series of investigations and experiments began into water-tight and water-resistant watches. While there had been some experimentation into this arena in the late 1890s, no system had ever been perfected. In 1926, Hans Wilsdorf, the founder of Rolex set his sights on achieving the first water-tight watch. On Nov. 24, 1927, Switzerland made history when Mercedes Gleitze wore a Rolex Oyster watch on her

Left: In 1880, IWC introduced its first digital watch. It featured a digital hour readout at 12, a digital minute readout in the center of the dial, and a subsidiary seconds hand at 6.

Below: This exceptional pocket watch from Ulysse Nardin dates to 1893. It features minute repeating chronometer with chronograph that was made especially for the Chicago Exhibition of 1893.

Bottom left: This chronograph, Breitling's Duograph with sweephand function, was created in 1946.

Top: Utilizing a gold Lépine movement, no. 2010, this Audemars Piguet watch features a minute repeater, perpetual calendar, leap years, moon phase and chronograph with center 60-minute counter that was added later. (circa 1882). Second photo reveals under-dial views of the perpetual calendar and moon phase.

Center right: The Hamilton Ventura is a recreation of the world's first electric watch and is a signature timepiece in Hamilton's American Classic collection since its introduction in 1957. This is an accurate design replica, but with an updated Swiss Quartz movement.

Bottom right: In 1960, a specially made Rolex Oyster similar to this was produced for Professor Jacques Piccard. It was strapped to the outside of his bathyscaphe, the Trieste, and submerged in the Pacific Ocean to a depth of 10,908 meters.

swim across the English Channel. After more than 10 hours in the water, it maintained perfect time with no moisture penetration. Wilsdorf aptly named this timepiece — considered the first truly tested water-resistant watch — the Oyster.

About a decade later, water-resistant watches underwent extensive scrutiny and testing. In 1936, an American explorer wore the Omega Marine diving watch to a depth of 73 meters (approximately 220 feet) in Lake Léman in Switzerland. And in 1960, a specially made Rolex Oyster reached new depths of water resistancy while strapped to a bathyscaphe, named the Trieste, which was submerged more than 10,000 meters into the Marianas Trench in the Pacific Ocean.

In 1969, a Swiss watch made history by traveling in the opposite direction. On July 21, 1969, astronaut Neil Armstrong wore an Omega Speedmaster as he stepped foot on the moon. Years later, in 1970, on the Apollo 13 mission, Omega's Speedmaster helped the crew avert a disaster. When an oxygen tank exploded the mission was critically jeopardized. The accuracy of the Omega watch played a critical role in assisting astronauts. With their instrument panel timing device inoperable, the Speedmaster enabled the module pilots to fire their rocket engine at just the right moment necessary so they could return to Earth safely.

The 20th century also ushered in experimentation with different power sources. In 1929 the first quartz crystal clock was made by Horton and Marrison in the United States. The first quartz watch, however, would not be developed until decades later. The first Caesium atomic clock was invented by Dr. Essen of the National Physical Laboratory in 1955. The atomic clock keeps time to within a few seconds every 100,000 years.

In 1957, America's Hamilton watch Company produced the first successful electric watch, powered by a battery. This watch, which was 10 years in the making, eliminated the mainspring by substituting an "energizer" or battery. Around the same time, a Swiss electronics engineer employed by Bulova Watch Company had the idea of using a vibrating tuning fork to power a watch. The Accutron Tuning fork watch (which uses an inch-long tuning fork instead of an escapement to power the oscillating circuit) was born.

In 1967, the Centre Electronique Horloger in

Neuchatel developed the first quartz wrist-watch (Beta 21). However, Switzerland did not believe that the world would want to see it produce a non-mechanical, inexpensive timepiece and watchmakers did not embrace or pursue the concept. In the 1970s, the Japanese began manufacturing quartz watches in droves. Customers flocked to stores for these flatter, easier-to-use quartz timepieces, dealing a nearly fatal blow to Swiss watch sales. This staggering impact put the Swiss watch industry immediately on a sickbed and many Swiss watch firms realized the need to compete, and took hold of quartz.

The arrival and acceptance of quartz on the market made design possibilities endless because of the flatness of the quartz crystal. In 1980, the world's thinnest wristwatch was created by Concord watch company. Called the Delirium IV, the wristwatch was crafted in 18-karat gold and measured .0385 of an inch. The watch retailed for $16,000 — bringing the concept of quartz watches to a higher realm.

Today, although some Swiss watch companies utilize quartz powered movements, the country is revered for its dedication to preserving the mechanical timepiece as one of the finest works of art and technical prowess in the world. As we emerge more fully onto the stage of international business travel and jetsetting, Swiss watchmakers are earnestly working to perfect new patents in wristwatches that will be relative to life in the 21st century.

Top left: In 1969, Omega was the first watch worn on the moon. Since 1965, it the Omega Speedmaster has accompanied all of the Apollo missions as the official chronograph. Seen here is Edwin "Buzz" Aldrin on the moon with his Omega strapped on the right wrist.

Left and right: Thinness was achieved in its ultimate glory in 1980 when Concord Watch Company created the world's thinnest wristwatch, the Delirium IV, which was .0385 of an inch thick.

Center left: Breitling's Chronomat-Chrono-Matic watch, circa 1970, features a patented bezel system, and telemetric scale.

Bottom: Called the clock that lives on air, the Atmos Clock by Jaeger-LeCoultre was devised in 1928. It operates on a mixture of gas and liquid that react to the air temperature, and keep the clock running. It is so accurate that it will suffer a cumulative loss of one day in 3,821 years.

Welcomed Complications

Usually when things are complicated, it means more work, more effort and more emotional strain, but in the end, it's worth it. The same is true of complicated watches. The highest achievements in watchmaking and technology, complicated timepieces transcend all realms of art and talent. These are timepieces inspired by artisans who put everything short of their actual lifeblood into the making of one watch. It is difficult to fathom the painstakingly minute and intricate work involved in designing these watches and seeing them through to fruition, which can take years. A novelty to the majority of watch lovers, these timepieces are recognized by those in the know as a treasure worth more than their weight in gold. While their true artistic value cannot be measured, typically at least 75 percent of the value of complicated watches comes from what's inside. Prized from generation to generation, some of the most intriguing watches in the world are astoundingly complex timepieces with multiple functions of distinction.

Previous pages: page 34: The inside of a Breguet complicated timepiece. The 21-jeweled tourbillon movement is hand etched to perfection. Page 35: From the inventor of the tourbillon and the forefather of modern watchmaking, this Breguet open-worked jewelry tourbillon is a masterpiece of art and craftsmanship. Created in 18K white gold, the bezel features flawless baguette-shaped Top Wesselton diamonds.

Above: One of the slimmest tourbillons in the world, Blancpain's tourbillon has a power reserve of eight days. The tourbillon movement is composed of 195 finely decorated and hand-assembled pieces.

Far right: This tourbillon timepiece from Robergé is called Androméde II. Crafted in 18K gold, the dial features pavé set diamonds, with a smaller time-telling subdial at 12.

Right: This Central Tourbillon watch from Omega features a self-winding movement and metalized hour and minute hands painted on two revolving sapphire crystals. The bezel is set with 48 Top Wesselton diamonds and the bracelet is set with 276 Top Wesselton diamonds, for a total weight of more than 37 carats.

To grasp the inherent value of and passion for complicated watches, one must first understand exactly what constitutes complicated timepieces. Such watches feature a variety of functions in addition to telling the time. Most feature one or two functions — but the watches can, and usually do, comprise many functions. The five most prized marks in watchmaking include the tourbillon, minute repeater, perpetual calendar, moon phase and equation of time. The degree of complexity involved in creating the different functions and bringing them together in one watch plays a vital role in determining which watches are the most complicated, and ultimately, most coveted.

The real love of a complicated watch arises from a profound respect for the craftsmanship and knowledge that in today's world of mass production, the watches are created by one master of technical knowledge and old-world skills.

The maker of a complicated timepiece offers it with great affection and pride — and usually tracks it like one watches after a baby or toddler. Most of the finest houses of watchmaking keep ledgers and binders in which they record the original sale of each prized watch and, where possible, any subsequent sales. After all, there are only a small number of these ingenious works created annually.

A majority of the most complex watches are collector items, and many — by the sheer nature of the craftsmanship involved in making one watch — command years of patient waiting by the customer before they are delivered. Those years of waiting, though, are filled with anticipation.

Indeed, realization that one will soon be owning one of the most exclusive watches in the world is, for many, a dream come true.

Tempting Tourbillons

Acclaimed by the world's top watchmakers as the movement perhaps most indicative of ultimate skill, the tourbillon is a masterpiece in art and technical prowess. The tourbillon, the French word for "whirlwind," is a highly precise movement that works as beautifully as it sounds (TUR bee ohn).

Conceived of by watchmaking legend Abraham-Louis Breguet in 1795, though not patented until 1801 and not marketed until 1805, the tourbillon regulator is a device intended to eliminate errors in timekeeping caused by the force of gravity when the watch is in certain positions. A watch runs at a slight difference in the horizontal and vertical positions, and errors of as much as a second a day can be caused by a flick of the wrist or the positioning of

Above left: Built to celebrate Girard-Perregaux's 200th anniversary is the Tourbillon with three gold Bridges in wristwatch format. In the background is the 1982 Tourbillon with three gold Bridges pocket watch.

Above right: Creator of the Tourbillon with three gold Bridges, venerable watchmaker Girard-Perregaux also works in other complications. This exquisite timepiece is a minute repeater.

Left: Considered the superlative complicated work of Chopard, this perpetual calendar timepiece features 437 individually hand-polished pieces. More than one year in the making, Chopard will create only three numbered series of 50 each in platinum, yellow gold and rose gold.

Above: Even the inside of a Chopard complicated timepiece is elegantly decorated. This tourbillon movement is hand etched to perfection.

Above: Franck Muller's Imperial Tourbillon with visible tourbillon is crafted in 18K gold and features a small seconds counter.

Top right: This elegantly decorated timepiece is a Daniel Roth masterpiece. It features a tourbillon window and triple rows of diamonds on the case and bezel.

Right: Containing the patented Franck Muller tourbillon, this Caliber '95 watch features a split-seconds chronograph with hours, minutes and center-seconds, a perpetual calendar with date, day of week, month and retrograde monthly equation, indicator of leap year, 24-hour meter, moon phase and indication of internal temperature of the watch. What's more, it features two sides so that it can easily convert from day to night.

the watch. The tourbillon compensates for these differences. In a tourbillon, the entire escapement (the device that regulates power in a mechanical timepiece) is fitted into a case or carriage and the complete assembly revolves continuously at the rate of one time per minute.

Prior to the tourbillon, the escapement and balance spring were mounted rigidly onto the main plate of mechanical wristwatches. Noting this to be a key contributor to inaccurate timekeeping, Breguet — driven to correcting even the slightest errors — created a construction wherein the balance and escapement are mounted on a movable platform geared to the third wheel. With the recurrent rotation and subsequent averaging out of the affects of gravity over one revolution of the carriage, the errors resulting from the effect are averaged out so that they, in effect, cancel each other out.

Even today, with progressions in technology and watchmaking, the tourbillon is considered one of the most precise, efficient timekeepers available. Demanding unsurpassed standards of craftsmanship, tourbillons are very costly and can take as long as six months to produce. They are created in extremely limited numbers by little more than a handful of watch companies. Leading the field with the creation of timepieces thought to be among the most complex in the world are Patek Philippe with its Caliber '89, Blancpain and the 1735, and IWC, International Watch Company, with

the Il Destriero Scafusia.

Watchmaking great Patek Philippe began work on its first tourbillon on October 21, 1864 and completed it six months later. From then on, the tourbillon and Patek Philippe sparked a romance that has never died. Relentless in its quest for perfection — with the highest standards of horology in place — Patek Philippe succeeded in 1989 of marking its 150th birthday with what has the distinction of being the most complicated timepiece in the world: Caliber '89. This pocket watch houses the tourbillon, along with a myriad of complicated functions and displays. A superior expression of the genius of watchmaking, the timepiece comprises 1,728 individual parts, two main dials, eight discs and 24 hands.

Among the 33 functions it offers are the hours, minutes and seconds in sidereal time (based on the earth's rotation), the times of sunset and sunrise, the equation of time, time in a different zone

Below: The crowning glory of Patek Philippe and complicated watchmaking in total is the Caliber '89 – the world's most complicated watch. Cited in the Guinness Book of Records as the world's most expensive watch (it sold at auction in 1989 for approximately $3.2 million), the Caliber '89 offers 33 different functions and displays.

Above: Cartier's exquisite Pasha timepiece is ensconsed in rows of sapphires. These stones lavishly cover the bracelet and bezel. The watch features a tourbillon and power reserve.

Right: Breguet, credited with creating the "perpetuelle" watch, began work on this masterpiece in 1787. This repeating watch features a power reserve, moon phase and subsidiary seconds dial. It sold in 1794.

Bottom right: Vacheron Constantin's preeminence in the luxury watch world is furthered by its continued production of such wondrous timepieces as this skeleton version of the minute repeater. Cased in 18K pink gold, this hand wound mechanical movement is extra thin and decorated by hand.

and split-second timing. What's more, the watch features the tourbillon escapement, the perpetual and secular calendar, an astronomical calendar, the celestial chart, the date of Easter, the moon phase, a split-seconds chronograph, a minute repeater, the Grand Strike and Small Strike, an alarm, a power reserve indicator and four-way setting system.

If this is not enough — there is more. Indeed, this watch, which underwent four years in the development stage and five years in the hand-assembly stage, features several additional functions and complications in the horological sense and offers one non-horological feature: a thermometer. With all of this packed into one timepiece, it's no wonder the first of its kind sold in excess of $3.2 million at a Geneva auction the same year it was created, thereby leading to its status in the Guinness Book of Records as the most expensive watch in the world.

While many companies find it difficult to measure up to the horological distinction of Caliber '89, watchmakers have not wavered in their conquest of complications. Indeed, this challenge has become the life work for many watchmakers in pursuit of perfection: Girard-Perregaux, IWC, Audemars Piguet, Vacheron Constantin, Franck Muller and a handful of others.

Girard-Perregaux's stellar contribution to the world of tourbillons came in the middle of the 19th century in the form of the now celebrated Tourbillon with three gold Bridges. The masterpiece won several prizes and distinctions over the years, including two gold medals at the Paris Exhibitions in 1867 and 1889.

Almost a century later, in 1981, Girard-Perregaux's master watchmakers reconceptualized the tourbillon's production and set about making an exact replica of the original 19th-century tourbillon with three gold Bridges. After successfully mastering this challenge in the form of a pocket watch, Girard-Perregaux next set out to miniaturize the format and present the Tourbillon with three gold Bridges in wristwatch format. Since then, the company has proudly introduced magnificent new tourbillons annually.

Another impressive tourbillon can be found in one of the world's most complicated wristwatches — the Il Destriero Scafusia by IWC. This watch in itself is a horological feat of accomplishment in the world of complex movements and technical prowess. The Il Destriero's movement consists of 750 parts and has a total of 21 functions and displays. The Il Destriero, dubbed the "warhorse," features a tourbillon, perpetual calendar, split-seconds chronograph with flyback hand, perpetual moon phase and extravagant minute repeater.

One of IWC's crowning achievements, the Il Destriero's tourbillon is a type of escapement that essentially revolves around itself and resists the pull of gravity. Called the flying tourbillon, the tourbillon is mounted on bearings on one side and is the first to complete eight vibrations per second, guaranteeing maximum precision. The escapement was also relieved of the effects of magnetism, as the tourbillon cage is made of anti-magnetic titanium. The ball bearing-mounted flying tourbillon consists of more than 80 single parts yet weighs less than .03 grams.

Watchmaking venerable Vacheron Constantin insists on the best in its tourbillons and has made a specialty of offering its complexities in skeletonized form so that the wearer, and onlookers, get more than an eyeful. One of the most stunning tourbillons is the open worked tourbillon from Vacheron Constantin's Les Complications collection. This complicated watch features a movement with twin series-coupled barrels. The skeletonizing of the watch movement required watchmakers to remove more than 70 percent of the movement's original metal before they could house the masterpiece in an 18-karat pink gold case.

Franck Muller, who patented his

Above: The back of the Il Destriero reveals the tourbillon movement.

Left: Combining so much more than the tourbillon, minute repeater and perpetual calendar into one timepiece, IWC has created one of the world's most complicated wristwatches in the Il Destriero Scafusia. Dubbed the Warhorse, this watch – which offers 21 different functions and displays – holds 760 mechanical parts and 77 jewels in the movement. Only 125 pieces will ever be created.

Above right: Only one example of this Audemars Piguet Grande Complication pocket watch exists. Its movement features 416 parts and 37 rubies. The setting features 288 diamond brilliants, 96 baguette diamonds, six baguette emeralds and six cabochon emeralds for a total weight of 47.45 carats. The watch offers 12 functions including day, date, month, and moon phase indicators, perpetual calendar with leap year, chronograph with flyback hand and a minute repeater.

Right: Bringing together the beauty of the minute repeater with the luxurious elegance of platinum, Patek Philippe's Ref. 5029 is a chronometer equipped with an ultra-thin R 27PS caliber movement. This movement is distinguished by the purity of its high-quality acoustic steel gongs and totally silent regulator. The case back features a cover with an anti-dust hinge that opens to reveal the movement through a sapphire crystal back. This watch is produced in a limited edition of 10 pieces only as a Commemoration 1997 of the opening of Patek Philippe's new workshops in Geneva.

own tourbillon, is master of several intricate and elaborate world premiers. Included among them, the Caliber 95, which features a patented Franck Muller tourbillon, a split-second chronograph, a perpetual calendar with date, day of the week, month and retrograde monthly equation, indication of leap years, 24-hour meter, moon phase and indication of internal temperature of the mechanism. What's more this unique watch is double faced, offering a true day-to-night watch.

Musical Magic

While so many complicated timepieces offer unrivaled beauty in their craftsmanship and precision, none can offer the special beauty that sonneries and repeaters offer — music to the ears. Equally as exacting in precision as any complicated watch movement, the repeaters and sonneries are in a class by themselves. These incredible instruments offer the soothing elegance of chimes to indicate the time.

A repeater is a watch with a striking mechanism that is activated at will by the wearer. With the push of a button or the move of a slide, the time is told by separate gonging or chiming sounds of different tones. Essentially, a very complex mechanical memory allows this timepiece to operate.

There are quarter repeaters in which the last hour and the quarter hour are indicated using two different pitched tones. There also are minute repeaters in which the hour, quarters and the minutes are sounded, half-quarter repeaters in which the hour, quarters and nearest half hours are sounded, and there are five minute repeaters in which the last hour, the quarters and one blow for each

five minutes past the last quarter are sounded. As a result of different hammers striking gongs in contrasting reverberations, each strike of hours, quarters and minutes has its own distinct sound.

Working on a similar system are Grande Sonneries. The sonnerie is a type of repeater that strikes the hours and quarter hours regularly at each quarter without the wearer needing to press a button. Also known as "Strikes," these watches can be found in grande strikes that chime the hours and the quarters and petite strikes that chime only the hours.

Interestingly, the initial mechanism utilized in sonneries and repeaters is derived from the chiming systems used in clocks and clock towers of centuries past. It is believed that it was not until about 1687 that English watchmaker Daniel Quare succeeded in applying a repeater mechanism to watches.

While repeating watches were in use as early as 1687, prior to 1750, the repeating mechanism sounded the hours and quarters on a bell fixed to the back of the case. There were some inherent problems with early minute repeaters in that if the pusher was not pushed all the way the time was not struck correctly. This led to the device known as an all-or-nothing piece which, in turn, led to surety in time-telling of minute repeaters.

Though intrinsically beautiful and melodic, their purpose was initially func-

Above: It seems the most complex watches are those the watchmaking greats often want to adorn in precious attire. This phenomenal Piaget timepiece is marvelous to look at and to listen to. The one-of-a-kind minute repeater is bedecked in nearly 23 carats of diamonds. Created for the 120th anniversary, this $1.5 million marvel is also a split-seconds chronograph.

tional. The chimes enabled wearers to learn the time at any hour of the day or night, without having to light a candle or oil lamp. The development of electricity, then, should have rendered the minute repeater obsolete. However, the sheer uniqueness and ethereal qualities of this type of watch have made it a coveted attraction. Watchmakers insist on perfecting the sounds of sonneries and repeaters. Some repeaters utilize the Westminster chimes for the ultimate in sound, while others use similar chime systems or bell systems. Watches that sound the time are a favorite among watchmakers. In fact, this is perhaps the one complication most frequently chosen to be adorned with diamonds and gemstones in an effort to make the timepiece as visually arresting and precious as it sounds to the ear.

In fact, Audemars Piguet's 1997 Grande Complication brought together in its 416 parts not only the minute repeater, split-second chronograph and perpetual calendar with moon phase, but also 288 brilliant diamonds, 96 baguette diamonds, 86 baguette emeralds and six cabochon emeralds — all for a total weight of nearly 50 carats.

Franck Muller, too, has ensconced some of his masterpieces with minute repeater in diamond bezels and decoration. The Caliber '97 not only introduced a new realm of music because of the use of different alloys, but is also elegantly set with baguette- and brilliant-cut diamonds. This timepiece introduces an original bell chime found in a pocket watch. In this design, two hammers strike the inside of the bell and produce a high and low sound. The watch also offers a new "silent mode" indicator on the dial so the user can silence the automatic chiming if he so chooses.

Other inventions and improvements on the minute repeaters come in new slide mechanisms, superbly enhanced protective structures (that ensure all or nothing-at-all striking) and improved metallurgical techniques with more sophisticated acoustics for more elaborate striking systems.

46

Left: From master watchmaker Franck Muller, this complex mechanical timepiece features a minute repeater that strikes the hours, quarters and minutes, perpetual calendar with retrograde monthly equation of time, leap year, 24 hours counter, moon phase, and a split-seconds chronograph with pulsometer. It is encased in solid platinum.

Perpetual Pleasure

Attesting to man's insatiable desire to measure and track time is the perpetual calendar watch. The perpetual calendar tracks and displays automatically, the day, month, date and the phases of the moon, adjusting for short months and leap years.

Calendar systems in timepieces are almost as old as watches themselves. In fact, there exists a watch made in England in the late 16th century that has a miniature calendar built into the timepiece. Many calendar watches took their inspiration directly from astronomical clocks and bell towers of the 15th and 16th centuries. Since then, calendars remained important functions in timepieces.

Watchmakers of the 1700s and early 1800s wrestled with obstacles inherent in calendar watches, such as how to automatically advance the date or find a system that would allow for leap years, indicating an interest in perpetual calendar watches as

much as 200 years ago. The development of the perpetual calendar system is generally credited to Louis Audemars in the year 1853, though the original development was not realized until 1860. The original system devised, and since perfected by several companies, features a circular cam consisting of 48 months accounting for differences in dates.

To date, perpetual calendars have come a long way. Many offer precision for hundreds of years with just one or two adjustments. Others offer smaller time frame precision with no adjustments. The selection and options available are numerous.

Patek Philippe has developed a secular perpetual calendar that runs on the full 400-years cycle of the Gregorian calendar and never needs resetting. A wheel in the movement makes just one revolution every four centuries.

Blancpain's perpetual calendar requires a minor one-day correction to the masterpiece just once early in the year 2100 — representing a perpetual calendar efficient for more than 200 years. This is the same technology utilized in Blancpain's mastery of complication, the 1735. In fact, the 1735 combines six master movements of the horological art into one watch: the ultra-slim mechanical movement, the perpetual calendar, moon phase, tourbillon, minute repeater and split-seconds chronograph.

Below: Number four of the Concord Mariner V Centenario series, this platinum piece features subdials that display the month, day, date and moon phase. The watch houses a minute repeater, tourbillon and thermometer.

Above: Recognizing the importance of perpetual calendars, Jaeger-LeCoultre's Master Perpetual is crafted only in platinum and produced in a limited edition of 250 pieces. The deep blue dial displays the hours, minutes, seconds, date, day of the week, month, year, decade and moon phase. The watch features the mechanical automatic movement, Jaeger-LeCoultre caliber 889/440/2.

Above right: Concord's Saratoga Exor is a unique work of art, inside and out. It is embellished with nearly 100 diamonds weighing more than 15 carats and features a tourbillon, minute repeater, perpetual calendar, moon phase and thermometer.

Right: The phases of the moon is a particular specialty of Blancpain. This automatic model is thought to be the smallest of its kind that indicates the moon phase, day, month and date.

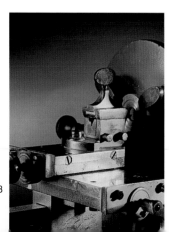

Moon Phase and Equation of Time

Other key complex functions that add to the fascination of complicated watchmaking and typically are associated with the calendar, include the moon phase and the equation of time. Perhaps the most self-explanatory of all complications, the moon phase shows the phases of the moon. It operates via a small disk within the case that holds the phases of the moon. As the disk rotates it reveals the proper moon phase for the progressing month. The wearer views the phases of the moon via a window aperture on the dial. Moon phases are one of the most telling aspects of man's fascination with astronomy, the sun and the moon.

Perhaps one of the most stunning renditions of the phases of the moon comes in the Grande Complication from venerable watchmaker Vacheron Constantin.

In this extraordinary pocket watch, which includes perpetual calendar, split seconds chronograph, minute repeater and alarm, the phases of the moon dial is crafted in elegant lapis lazuli. Bringing together the moon phase with the intrigue of the sun, moon and planets, Ulysse Nardin has some of the most unusual astronomical configurations on some of its watches, including the Planetarium Copernicus — cited in the Guinness Book of Records for its astronomical clock face. This watch by Ulysse Nardin gives a view of the entire solar system from the vantage point of the North Pole. In addition to the moon phase, the self-winding Copernicus offers the exact astronomical positions of the sun, moon and the planets Mercury, Mars, Venus, Jupiter and Saturn.

Another key function sometimes found in watches with perpetual calendars is the more complicated equation of time. One of the most difficult complications to put into a wristwatch, the equation of time is based on sun time. Because time is not consistent from one day to the next in relation to the meridian, an average day was

fixed. The duration of an average day — also called an average sun day — was calculated based on the average of all the days in the year. Its duration does not vary; it is consistently 24 hours.

The true sun day is the interval of time that passes between two consecutive passages of the sun at the meridian. This time can vary from 14 minutes and 20 seconds to 16 minutes and 23 seconds on certain days of the year. The equation of time essentially indicates the difference between the time of a true sun day and an average sun day.

Again a representation of the correlation between man, earth and the sun, the general principal of equations of time date back centuries. It is only with the technological advancements and miniaturization of movements that these calculations can be fitted into a watch. It is with this adherence to precision, craftsmanship and technology in mind that the world's greatest watchmakers bring life and breath to the art of timekeeping. Every work of art considered a complicated watch is an example of magnificence. Indeed, a glance at these marvels brings to full light the saying: "Good things are worth waiting for."

Above: Vacheron Constantin's heritage and technical prowess come together in this Grande Complication timepiece, 1928.

Left: Creation of the movement is a tedious job. Every piece is fitted together with the utmost of care. Shown here is a Breguet moon phase watch in the making.

Bottom: Distinctively Audemars Piguet, this skeletonized Royal Oak is a masterpiece featuring perpetual calendar, moon phase display.

Split Second Timing

As EVERY SECOND becomes more and more important, the best master watchmakers make sure we can measure those seconds to the tiniest fractions in an array of chronographs that enable us to track time in intervals. With all of its fancy subdials and intricate faces, the chronograph has become a necessity in this fast-paced world. The word "chronograph" is derived from the Greek words "chronos" meaning time and "grapho" meaning I write, but time writer is the common translation. A chronograph is a watch that not only indicates the time of day, but also is equipped with a mechanism that makes it possible to measure continuous or discontinuous intervals of time, without affecting the time-telling functions. Often those intervals are from the tiniest fraction of a second up to 12 hours, depending on the chronograph. Essentially the wearer can push a button on the case to set a separate hand of the watch in motion, stop it and have it return to zero when finished timing the event.

Breitling

Previous pages: Breitling has a distinguished history in the world of chronograph development and sports timing. This Crosswind super chronograph is equipped with a high frequency 28,800 vibrations-per-hour self-winding chronograph movement. It features a tachometer ring and 120-position notched track ratchet bezel.

Above: The Type XX Aeronavale Breguet chronograph in pink gold features a flyback function and self-winding movement.

Above right: Chopard's Mille Miglia chronograph was designed to celebrate the 70th anniversary of this legendary automobile race. It features a tachometer, date window and hour and 30-minute counters. The independent small seconds counter is decorated with the arrow that is the race's emblem.

Right: The Omega Speedmaster, a master of records. This model is an automatic day-date am/pm chronograph in pink gold. For subtle elegance and simple use, the chronograph features 30-minute counter at 12 and 12-hour counter at 6.

Below: Blancpain's new self-winding Chronograph 2185 features a 40-hour power reserve, and offers seconds, 30-minutes and 12-hour totalizers.

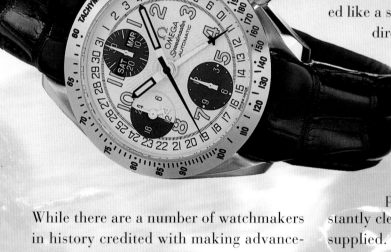

While there are a number of watchmakers in history credited with making advancements in chronographs, it is English watchmaker George Graham who is generally credited with creating a mechanism in 1720 (though, not a watch) to measure small intervals of time. The first-of-its-kind mechanism used weights and a pendulum. The hand of the mechanism divided the second into four segments.

More than a century later, in 1821, Nicolas Rieussec announced his invention of the true chronograph, which recorded intervals of time. In fact, the first chronograph clock was invented by Rieussec in 1822 and actually wrote the time to be measured on the dial. It had a hand constructed like a small pen that marked an ink spot directly on the dial at the beginning and at the end of the measuring process. The distance between the two dots represented the time that passed between starting and stopping. Unfortunately, this chronograph clock had inherent problems — the dial had to be constantly cleaned and ink had to be regularly supplied. Still, Rieussec's invention set the world's watchmakers on a race to perfect the chronograph.

Hundreds of designs and patents in chronograph technology emerged. While pocket watches were built with second hands that showed the elapsed time, they, too, had problems. The biggest obstacle was that the entire watch movement had to be stopped to use the second hand for timing events, so that in the end the correct time-keeping function was lost each time something was measured. But ongoing investigations and inventions sparked further

perfection of chronographs, so that finally the movement was perfected and the time measurement function could run independently of the timekeeping functions.

In 1840, Adolphe Nicole, a Swiss horologist living in England, took out a patent for a device that let the user set the seconds hand back to zero — thereby introducing the three functions of the modern day chronograph (start, stop and reset to zero). It was not until 1862, though, that Nicole, working in conjunction with Henri-Féréol Piquet, exhibited a chronograph that could start, stop and reset to zero without disturbing the clockwork mechanism. Eight years later, in 1870, Joseph Winnerl of Paris, introduced the first forerunner of today's split-second chronograph in a pocket watch. His watch featured two seconds hands, one on top of the other. One indicated the start

of the action and the other marked the end.

By the late 19th century, chronographs became commonplace in pocket watches. By 1882, chronographs already were appearing in the catalog of Edouard Heuer. By the turn of the century, it stood to reason that 20th century wristwatches would, of course, house chronographs. It was around 1910 that wristwatches started appearing on the market with chronographs movements. In 1913, Omega watch company had already advertised a chronograph wristwatch. In fact, Omega, Movado, Heuer, Rolex and Ulysse Nardin were among the first Swiss

Top left: This mechanical movement with manual wind-up chronograph from Franck Muller is called the Endurance 24. It is a limited edition timepiece with three counters and a tachometer on the bezel.

Above: From Baume & Mercier's Classima collection of chronographs, this automatic movement features 40-hour power reserve and a sweep seconds hand, 12-hour counter and 30-minute counter.

Left: The Havana automatic, ref. 5850 from Franck Muller, is a curved chronograph, a special feat in watchmaking. It features an automatic movement with platinum rotor. The 12-hours counter is at 9, the 30-minutes counter is at 3, and the seconds counter is at 6.

watch companies to produce wristwatch chronographs with the start, stop and return to zero function all achieved by a single pushpiece in the winding crown.

In 1934 Breitling first advertised a wrist chronograph design with two push buttons on the case. One button started and stopped the chronograph as often as desired

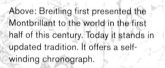

and the other moved the hand back to zero after the timing was stopped. This new mechanism became the standard of chronographs and was adopted by a majority of other watchmaking firms, as it was this mechanism that made it possible to time a multitude of separate intervals. In 1969, thanks to an alliance between Heuer, Hamilton-Buren and Breitling, the automatic chronograph was born.

Today's chronographs are easily recognizable because they typically have at least one smaller, constantly moving seconds hand, plus a larger manually operated second hand off of the center. Additionally, there typically is a small subsidiary dial with a minute counter to show elapsed time. Generally a push button is found on either side of the winding crown to operate the chronograph, and, in some chronographs, particularly split-seconds chronographs (also sometimes referred to by their French name: Rattrapantes), there is a third push button on the case.

The term split-seconds chronograph

Left: The new Omega Dynamic chronograph is inspired by a famous Omega pilot watch popular from 1930 to 1960. It is a self-winding mechanical chronograph with 60-second and 30-minute totalizers.

Bottom left: In daring colors of sport, Robergé's M31 chronograph measures elapsed times of 1/5th of a second by a mechanical movement that is linked to a quartz movement with date and small seconds.

Below: From Philippe Charriol, this elegant sport chronograph offers exciting color and exacting time.

is actually a misnomer, in that it does not split the second beyond the 1/5th or 1/10th of a second allowed by the mechanism, but instead, the hands split, or appear to divide.

A split-seconds chronograph has two second hands, one of which is usually directly beneath the other, so that when the timing device is not being used, the additional seconds hand is not visible; however, when the timing device is used, the two hands can split and act independently of one another.

Basically, a split-seconds chronograph allows the timing of several events starting at the same time, but each with a different duration. The first hand is started, stopped and reset with one push button; the other hand has its own push button. Generally, in a split-seconds chronograph the hands start together timing an event. When one particular portion (such as a lap) is complete, with the push of a button one hand (the split) stops while the other hand (the sweep) keeps on timing the event. After the time has been read from the

Above: An early player in the world of chronographs, Rolex continues today with its Oyster Perpetual Cosmograph Daytona timepiece. With or without diamonds, the watch is a gem in the world of sporty elegance.

Far right: Blancpain's Flyback chronograph is designed for contemporary lifestyles. This ladies' self-winding chronograph features a mechanism that allows a return-to-zero function at any time by the press of a button.

Below: Hublot's deep blue chronograph with Colonial mesh bracelet offers stunningly clean and elegant appeal.

split hand, another push of a button causes it to jump and join the other moving hand. Many chronographs also employ a flyback hand that enables the chronograph to time simultaneous events or actions. At the conclusion of the timing, the two hands return to zero by means of a flyback lever.

Over the years, hundreds of chronograph movements have been developed. Some have minute counters, and those that count longer times usually offer hour counters, which feature a separate subdial. Some chronographs feature a telemeter scale that offers a measurement of distances; others feature a tachometer for measurement of speeds and still others feature a pulsimeter to measure pulse frequency. Indeed, the

possibilities are endless: there are chronographs with hour registers and world time, with calculators, tide indications and tables, compasses and even breath registers.

A chronograph can also be a chronometer; however the two should not be confused. A chronometer is a clock or watch that has received a certificate after being tested and proven to have a prescribed degree of precision and efficiency according to stringent testing standards in the realm of temperatures, positions, etc. Any timepiece — not just

Center: TAG-Heuer's new 6,000 series of chronographs offers elegance and true professional instrumentation. This steel-and-blue timepiece offers single time measurement (a simple measure of elapsed time), additional time measurement (the ability to take a pause or time-out from time measurement), intermediate time (half-time readings), and two compared times (time of winner and second place competitor).

a chronograph — can be enrolled in testing for chronometer status.

Many chronographs offer calendars or moon phases; those that offer the perpetual calendar are considered among the most technically advanced chronographs. Patek Philippe was among the first to mount perpetual calendars on chronograph wristwatches. Thereafter, International Watch Company developed a setting mechanism that needs no correction apparatus, has a controlled moon phase, and can be set quickly.

The possibilities for other functions to be added to chronograph watches is vast, and dependent only upon the limits and constraints master watchmakers are bound to by the confines of their technical prowess and the physical size of the watch case.

While chronographs have played an important role in professional sports timing, they play an even more important role on the wrists of sports enthusiasts and watch lovers alike. Sports lovers utilize chrono-

Top left: Style de Chaumet chronograph in 18K gold features the start and stop function with the top push button and split-time and reset-to-zero with the bottom button.

Top: The Lindbergh Spirit collection by Longines is based on styling design from Lindbergh's suggestions to the firm. These colorful chronographs offer fresh appeal for the active lifestyle.

Above: Great aviators in time: Top photo Louis Blériot. Bottom: Charles Lindberg.

Left: Typical of Robergé's styling, the Andromède II chronograph measures time to 1/5th of a second and offers 30-minute and 12-hour counters. Its ergonomic steel case features a magnified date window.

Background: The Twinsixty from Breitling is a classic example of a chronograph wristwatch for use as an instrument. Ideally designed for displaying measured times of more than 60 minutes, the two distinct totalizer readouts allow the wearer to read elapsed times as he would on a standard watch dial. This self-winding chronograph features calendar and 24-hour readout, rotating bezel with circular slide rule, and measures short times to 1/5th second.

Right: Ref. 3970E from Patek Philippe is a manually wound wristwatch with chronograph and perpetual calendar with moon phase. A complicated watch and one of the highest technical chronographs to be made, this watch is one of a very few of its kind.

Far right: This Harry Winston chronograph features the Pulsimeter. It can compute cardiac rhythms, read directly on the pulsimetric graduations inscribed on the dial. The pulse is taken during 15 heartbeats upon pushing the special function button which, when pushed again, provides an instant readout of the cardiac rhythm. Each model features the Piguet 1185 self-winding movement.

graphs for timing practices or races, or for timing diving stints, aerobics routines, or other similar events. However, a vast majority of people wearing chronographs today do so simply because they love the look. With the active outdoor lifestyles people of the 90s, the chronograph offers a refined yet rugged appearance that is in high demand. Indeed, the subdials found on a chronograph have a sporty appeal that offers latitude in dressing, as well as in timing.

Whether the chronograph wristwatch is worn for its look or its performance

is — essentially — inconsequential. The reality is that it is a precise instrument that not only tells time, but allows timing of events — all from the wrist. Even a century ago, this was unfathomable to watchmakers, but with perserverance in the realm of technology, and persistance in the world of watchmaking, chronograph wristwatches are today one of the most popular trends. In fact, the 1990s can aptly be labeled the decade of the chronograph wristwatch.

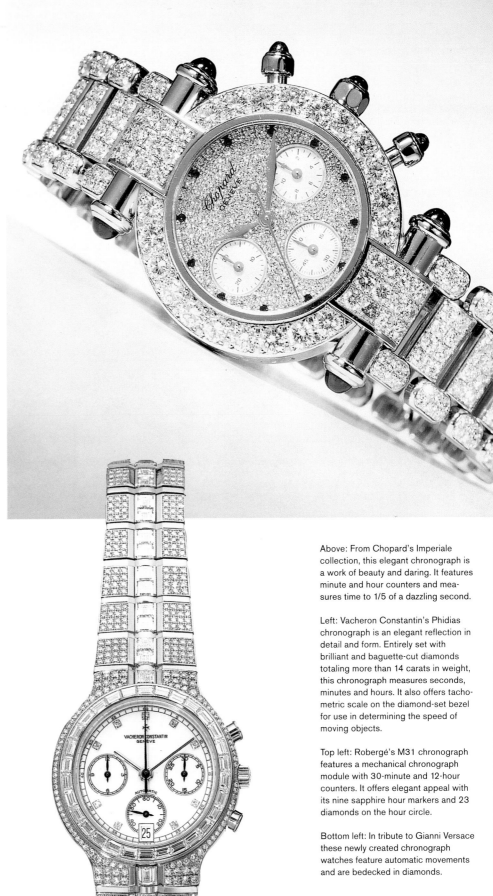

Above: From Chopard's Imperiale collection, this elegant chronograph is a work of beauty and daring. It features minute and hour counters and measures time to 1/5 of a dazzling second.

Left: Vacheron Constantin's Phidias chronograph is an elegant reflection in detail and form. Entirely set with brilliant and baguette-cut diamonds totaling more than 14 carats in weight, this chronograph measures seconds, minutes and hours. It also offers tachometric scale on the diamond-set bezel for use in determining the speed of moving objects.

Top left: Robergé's M31 chronograph features a mechanical chronograph module with 30-minute and 12-hour counters. It offers elegant appeal with its nine sapphire hour markers and 23 diamonds on the hour circle.

Bottom left: In tribute to Gianni Versace these newly created chronograph watches feature automatic movements and are bedecked in diamonds.

The Art of Time

PERHAPS MORE THAN any other art movement, Art Deco influenced and changed the shape of every facet of life. From Paris to America and around the world, leaders in Art Deco emerged as architects, painters, sculptors, fashion designers and great jewelry houses. Art Deco — a nebulous description at best — was an era wrought with expression and artistic distinction. The words Art Deco mean different things to different people, as the period encompassed a wealth of artistic modes spanning two decades, and infringing on nearly every spectrum of life. Art Deco — whose seeds were sown as early as the turn of the century — emerged first in the form of architecture, then stemmed quickly into interiors and home furnishings such as furniture, light fixtures, paintings, sculpture. It similarly encroached on home goods such as ceramics, pottery, porcelain, and glass, and then into the world of industrial design. Almost immediately, Art Deco leaped into the realm of fashion, accessories, and jewelry — all within a 20-year span.

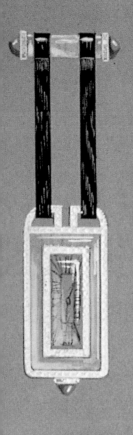

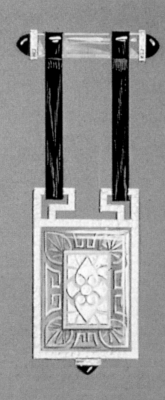

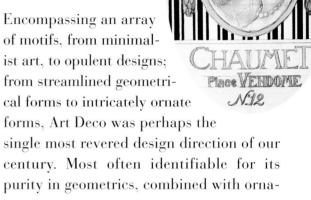

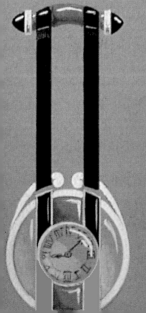

Encompassing an array of motifs, from minimalist art, to opulent designs; from streamlined geometrical forms to intricately ornate forms, Art Deco was perhaps the single most revered design direction of our century. Most often identifiable for its purity in geometrics, combined with orna-

mental elegance, the era of Art Deco was extraordinary.

Difficult to describe because of its contradictory final forms, the era first started with the abandonment of Art Nouveau,

Previous pages: page 60: Van Cleef & Arpels "Chatelaine" watch with pink diamonds, onyx and a hexagon-shaped diamond center, mounted in platinum. Page 61: From the "1930" collection of Van Cleef & Arpels timepieces, these three current watch models are recreations of the past. Geometrically inspired, the mini-ladies' watches feature diamonds and precious stones and ribbed satin watch straps reminiscent of the period.

Left: From Chaumet, these drawings from the Art Deco period illustrate various examples of diamond and onyx or enamel pendant watches.

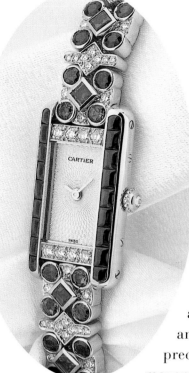

which had focused mostly on delicate and sinuous floral motifs. Art Deco was contrastingly modern, and originally brought into play clean designs in geometrical shapes. Later, the use of straight and curved lines played an important role, as did precise florals and languid movement. Most sculptures of the era— whether of people, nymphs, or animals — depicted movement: Birds took flight; people danced, embraced, or engaged in some other definitive pose; animals leapt and ran.

Indicative of this important architectural period are buildings such as Radio City Music Hall, or the Chrysler Building in New York. In industrial design, The Normandie Ocean liner, introduced to the world in 1935, epitomized the era with its sleek lines and opulent decor.

When the movement hit fashion, it

often ensconced in ermine collars high on the neck. Red, white and black dominated the color palette of the era. Later designs featured sleeker, more sensual dresses, but still with a flow at the very bottom, plunging necklines and equally plunging, or even

came by way of Paris, in styles rich in elegance. Women's clothing was, at first, fitted on top, flowing from the waistline and

bare, backs. Colors became decadent, bold, and sometimes outrageous in florals and patterns.

It was this styling that promulgated new design inspirations in jewelry. Throughout the 20-year Art Deco stint, jewelry featured one of three themes: stark geometrics; simple florals; dazzling combinations of brilliant precious gemstones and diamonds. Typically the designs were influenced by Egyptian, Oriental, Russian, or Middle Eastern motifs and colors.

So as not to be forgotten in an era of opulence, watches necessarily became bolder and more significant, flaunting mixes of circles, square, triangle and rectangles juxtaposed in abstract patterns. They emerged adorned in the richest rubies, emeralds, sapphires and diamonds in wonderful newly invented geometric cuts. Diamonds, too, were often mixed with such substances as onyx, coral, lapis lazuli, turquoise, jade and enamel for new looks in wristwatches.

While these wonderful timepieces were bolder in design, they varied in case size and shape. Initially larger, more significant pieces were created, and later, with sleeker styles in fashion, it became important to create smaller, slimmer timepieces. One important contributor to this stage of the era was Jaeger-LeCoultre, whose miniature Reverso

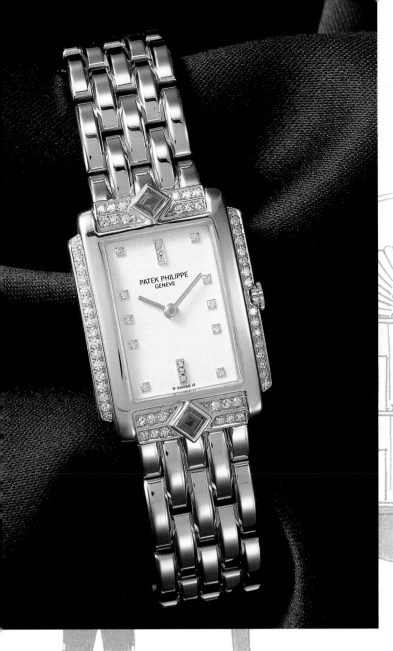

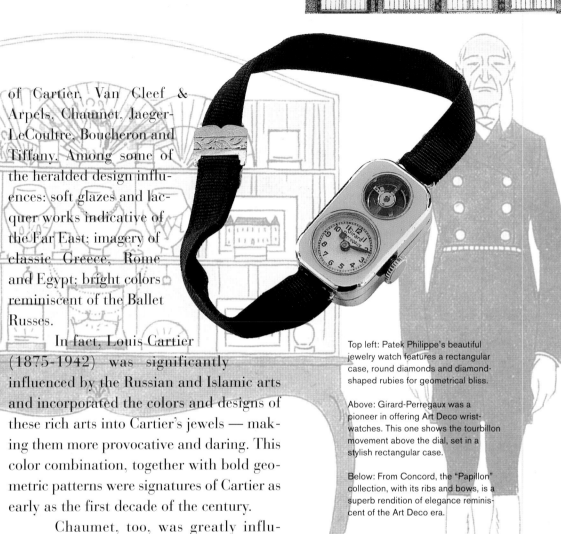

of Cartier, Van Cleef & Arpels, Chaumet, Jaeger-LeCoultre, Boucheron and Tiffany. Among some of the heralded design influences: soft glazes and lacquer works indicative of the Far East; imagery of classic Greece, Rome and Egypt; bright colors reminiscent of the Ballet Russes.

In fact, Louis Cartier (1875-1942) was significantly influenced by the Russian and Islamic arts and incorporated the colors and designs of these rich arts into Cartier's jewels — making them more provocative and daring. This color combination, together with bold geometric patterns were signatures of Cartier as early as the first decade of the century.

Chaumet, too, was greatly influ-

Top left: Patek Philippe's beautiful jewelry watch features a rectangular case, round diamonds and diamond-shaped rubies for geometrical bliss.

Above: Girard-Perregaux was a pioneer in offering Art Deco wristwatches. This one shows the tourbillon movement above the dial, set in a stylish rectangular case.

Below: From Concord, the "Papillon" collection, with its ribs and bows, is a superb rendition of elegance reminiscent of the Art Deco era.

watches were unequivocally Art Deco. Predominant case shapes were square, round and elliptical.

During this period, silk and braided cord became important as watch straps, predominantly in black or red. Later, when florals came into play, they were with great attention to realism and detail, and frequently sported gold bracelets. All meant to complement the fashions of the day, the wristwatches of this period continue to be emulated today.

Among the leaders in the realization of Art Deco watches were the great houses

enced by the striking Russian colors and lavish design appeal, and most often brought together dripping diamonds with brilliant rubies in uniquely lavish designs. During this period, Van Cleef & Arpels was similarly enthralled and turned to new variations of design, influenced by the riches unearthed from King Tutankhamun's tomb in 1922. Still, Van Cleef & Arpels remained faithful to the flower, its signature jewelry art form, and perfected new incredibly lustrous designs of florals motifs formed by geometrically cut stones. This wonderfully decadent period in socializing, dressing, and accessorizing came to a sensible slow-down with the impending onset of the Second World War — yielding new watch designs, albeit less opulent — that emphasized case shapes. Square-, rectangular- and barrel-shaped watch cases premiered as the leading design element.

In fact, this was the period that ushered in the overwhelming interest in tonneau-shaped watch cases, tank-shaped timepieces, and cushioned rectangulars. And these became the earmarks of the move from Art Deco to what today we refer to as the retro look of the 1940s.

Even today, watch manufacturers cannot turn their backs on the elegant, impressive styles of that bygone era. Many dabble in updated offerings based on designs of the period — either today's recreations from yesterday's archives, or new interpretations direct from imagination.

Opposite page: Designed by Baume & Mercier, circa 1940. Ladies' square-shaped watch.

Left: This ladies' tonneau-shaped wristwatch, made in 1925 by Movado, is set in platinum and adorned with diamonds. The tonneau shape was among the most popular of the era.

Below left: Called the Omega Golf, this timepiece from 1931 is a silver watch that slides into a leather-covered case.

Below: This wonderful Movado clock is crafted in blue enamel, onyx and diamonds and is fashioned in true Art Deco motif.

Bottom: In an elegant mix of jade and black enamel, this 1930 table clock from Van Cleef & Arpels designed with baguette diamonds once belonged to the Duchess of Windsor.

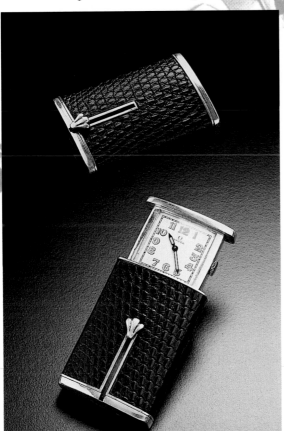

Enchanted Elegance

IN THE WORLD of watchmaking, certain arenas stand out from all others. Such is the case with the jewels of time — magnificent masterpieces transformed into objects of art with precious gems. Their purpose reaches beyond the utilitarian task of tracking time to captivating with their breathtaking beauty and allure. Perhaps nothing is as enchanting as the sparkling elegance of the finest gemstones in the world. And as craftsmen have learned to take these gems of the earth and brilliantly cut and polish them with increasing expertise, men and women alike have been caught up in their spell. Diamonds, rubies, sapphires, emeralds and pearls: over the centuries they have captivated and fascinated. They have adorned the robes, rings and challises of priests of many religions. They were worn by knights in the middle ages as emblems of luck, love and victory, and since antiquity, they have been in crowns and royal jewelry. It is only fitting that they grace technical masteries, enhancing the artistic genius of today's wristwatches.

Previous pages: page 69: In a stunning work of art and craftsmanship, Piaget's pendant watch is crafted in diamonds and emeralds for a scintillating effect. Page 68: This high jewelry watch from Piaget offers personality with its dazzling diamonds. Six rows of diamonds comprise the bracelet, and the watch dial matches in design.

Right: Working magnificent feats of beauty, Chopard brings diamonds to life in its Presence Collection.

Center: A finely executed jewelry watch from Breguet, featuring a gold mesh bracelet whose intricate pattern dates back to the chains designed centuries earlier by Breguet for pocket watches.

Gemstones have been revered as omens, protectors, and holders of great spiritual empowerment. Ancient myths and beliefs revolving around these stones are perhaps more plentiful than the stones themselves.

Prized and valued as symbols of wealth, power and opulence, gemstones hold their greatest allure and grandest glitter in their romantic appeal. Each of these gems has the overwhelming ability to tantalize and fascinate. This is perhaps the reason so many of the greatest watchmakers have been unable to resist using these stones in their creations.

It was in the 16th century that the first timepieces adorned with gemstones appeared. This was, no doubt, initially a reaction to John Calvin's ban against jewelry. Jewelers and goldsmiths, sanctioned from creating adornments, combined their efforts with clock makers and soon clocks and watches were bedecked in pearls, sapphires and diamonds. The watch was transformed from a utilitarian item to an exquisitely crafted piece of jewelry that also kept time.

The earliest watches typically featured gemstones on the bezel only, or sometimes a single jewel was inlaid in the center of the pocket

watch cover. Later, watches became even more lavish, especially as different members of European royalty began custom ordering watches to ensure they had a one-of-a-kind timepiece. Breguet created a bejeweled timepiece for Queen Marie-Antoinette of France that is still revered for its beauty and construction.

With the advent of thinner watch movements and quartz movements, ladies watches became even more popular. While watchmakers adorn men's watches with gemstones to a certain degree, it is the woman's watch that is typically lavished in riches.

Today the finest watch companies produce timepieces that feature diamonds, sapphires, rubies and emeralds

to almost unthinkable degrees. This use of gemstones is heralded as a fine art that enhances not only the value of a timepiece, but more importantly the uniqueness. These magnificent creations, referred to as Haute Joaillerie timepieces, command multitudes of stones, significant amounts of time in the making, and master hand craftsmanship.

Often gem cutters and setters work side by side to select and cut the finest stones, intrinsically perfect in their color and flawlessness. It is not unusual to find dozens, even hundreds of gemstones on a single timepiece.

The making of these entrancing masterpieces is a tedious and time consuming effort. Every single stone is hand-set by a skilled craftsman who can spend only a few hours a day at this close-up work. The creation of one timepiece requires hundreds of hours of a setter's time, and can take months, even years, to complete. But this painstaking process is rewarding, often giving birth to some of the most spectacular watches ever to be seen.

By the sheer nature of their craftsmanship and design (their creation relies on the availability of the right color, size and abundance of stones), a vast majority of jeweled timepieces are one-of-a-kind creations, or limited editions. Depending on the gemstones and the labor involved in producing each piece, a jeweled masterpiece can range in price from several thousand dollars to several million dollars. In fact, a high-jeweled masterpiece may well be the world's most expensive watch. In a feat of exceptional determination, Vacheron Constantin's master jewelers spent more than 6,000 hours creating the magnificent Kallista watch. Consisting of 118 diamonds and weighing 130 carats, the sumptuous timepiece is

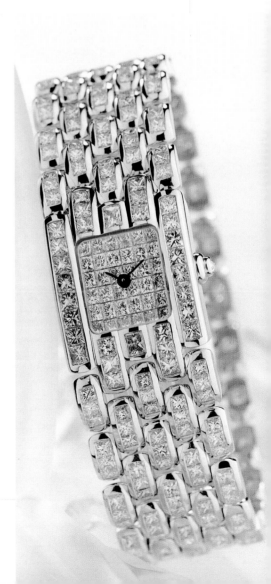

Above: From Patek Philippe's classical Ellipse collection, this timepiece is kissed with heart-shaped cabochon rubies weighing more than one carat each. Eight rubies are mounted in 18K gold to mark the hours on the mother-of-pearl dial.

Right: From the archives of Vacheron Constantin – the famous Kallista watch. Made in 1977, the watch was sculpted from a gold ingot and housed more than 130 carats of diamonds. It is valued at $9 million.

Bottom right: Stone setting is a tedious job, often requiring hundreds of hours of intense manual labor.

valued at $9 million.

While gemstones of lesser stature are sometimes utilized, it is primarily the rarest diamond, ruby, emerald and sapphire that adorns jeweled watches. Rubies, and sometimes sapphires, are also found within certain mechanical movements. It was quite some time ago that watchmakers began utilizing rubies as part of the watch movement. It was found that these stones, used as bearings for gears instead of metal, reduced friction.

However, it is on the outside of high-jeweled watches — on the case, bracelet, dial or bezel — that gemstones offer luster and decorative appeal. An important factor in the overall beauty of a high-jeweled watch is the cut of the gemstone. There are a wealth of different cuts used on stones, but for watches, the most-used cuts are squares (carré), trapeze, brilliants (round), marquise, pear, baguette (rectangle) and an array of other fancy shapes. Pearls are also used in high jeweled watchmaking, but most often as bracelets — typically running in triple and quadruple strands. Sometimes pearls are found as an outer adornment rimming a pocket watch or other special timepiece, but because of their shape and the inability to set them in such a way that they would not be damaged by wear and tear, they are not as

frequently used on cases, bezels or dials.

The best jewels in the world are crafted in only the finest metals. High jeweled watches feature platinum as the first metal of choice, but 18-karat white, yellow and rose gold are often utilized and sometimes specifically chosen because of the play of color these metals offer. Beyond the caratage and number of gemstones, there is the setting. Often a variety of different stone setting techniques are used within the same jeweled timepiece. The most popular settings for jeweled watches, however, include bead or pavé setting —

Left: From Audemars Piguet, the Roberta line of exceptional ladies watches is inspired by nature, and utilizes a variety of stones, cuts, and settings to achieve its beauty. Brilliants, diamond-cut baguettes, pears, pavé-set Arabesques, emerald-cut baguettes are all used.

Below: Dubbed the Mini-Poesie for its delicate beauty, this unique work of art from Bertolucci is crafted in 18K white gold and features 36 baguette diamonds, 378 full-cut diamonds for a total weight of more than 15 carats. The two square emeralds weigh more than three carats.

Below right: Concord utilizes diamonds in its Saratoga Exor collection.

typically used for dials and bezels, and channel setting, which is often used on bezels and bracelets. In pavé settings, the stones are placed so closely together that the surface looks "paved" with gemstones. It is achieved by drilling tiny holes into the metal and dropping the stones into place using a tiny hand tool. In channel setting, the stones are neatly lined up and held in place between two tracks of gold to form a sleek row. Several great watch and jewelry making houses, such as Chopard and Van Cleef & Arpels, have perfected their own stone-setting techniques in watchmaking to offer some of the most breathtaking and scintillating jeweled timepieces.

One of the most innovative techniques is realized in Chopard's Happy Diamonds timepieces. Interestingly, what makes these watches so dazzling are its "unset" diamonds. In the early 1970s, one

of Chopard's top designers, inspired by the radiance and sparkle of diamonds, wanted to capture the beauty of diamonds as they are seen without a setting, which he felt concealed the gem's luster. His realization of this idea gave birth to what was to become an award winning wristwatch — and subsequent collection — for Chopard.

In these watches, loose diamonds are specially cut, its point covered with a thin layer of gold, then encased between two sapphire crystals, one directly covering the watch dial and the other the top crystal of the watch. The diamonds move freely with every move of the wrist. The brilliant innovation was an immediate success, so much so, in fact that the company has since established a complete Happy Diamonds jewelry and accessories line. Others have tried to emulate Chopard's grandeur in this loose-stone setting, but none have enjoyed the success

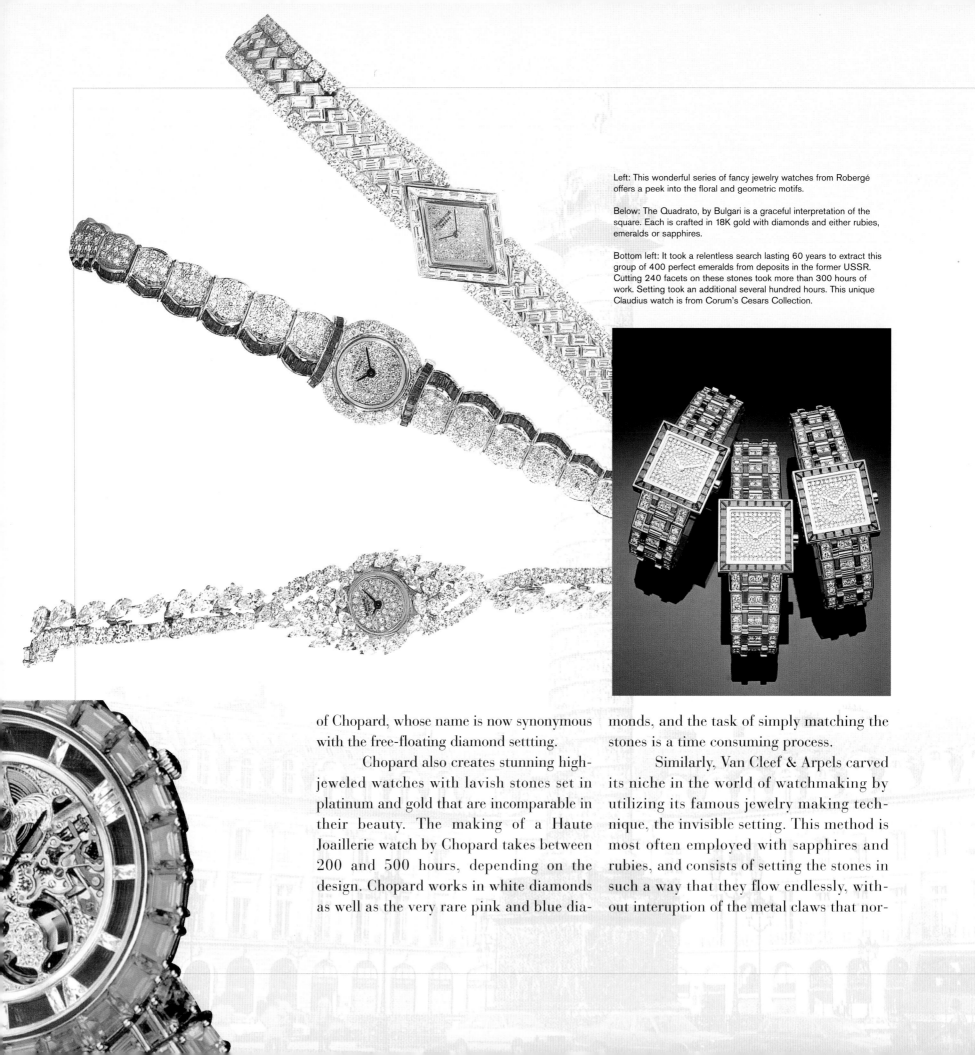

of Chopard, whose name is now synonymous with the free-floating diamond settting.

Chopard also creates stunning high-jeweled watches with lavish stones set in platinum and gold that are incomparable in their beauty. The making of a Haute Joaillerie watch by Chopard takes between 200 and 500 hours, depending on the design. Chopard works in white diamonds as well as the very rare pink and blue dia-

monds, and the task of simply matching the stones is a time consuming process.

Similarly, Van Cleef & Arpels carved its niche in the world of watchmaking by utilizing its famous jewelry making technique, the invisible setting. This method is most often employed with sapphires and rubies, and consists of setting the stones in such a way that they flow endlessly, without interuption of the metal claws that nor-

mally hold gems secure. Beneath the stones is a grid of gold or platinum threads onto which the stones, grooved on the backs, fit snugly. The interlocking cut and setting system essentially forces the stones into one another and holds them securely in place — creating a veritable seamless continuity of gems.

Combining this setting style with its love of floral motifs in some of its more elaborate jeweled watches, Van Cleef & Arpels offers some lusciously refreshing flower and garland timepieces in rubies, diamonds and emeralds.

In high jewelry watches, flora, as well as fauna, play an important role as themes. Many companies build their watch collection motifs around a certain type of flower, or garland, while others favor specific animals.

Cartier, for instance, is famed for its Panther motifs. Taking extreme care in placing a myriad of exquisite stones onto its high-jeweled watches, Cartier is an expert at achieving soft, supple, pliable bracelets ensconcing the hardest substance

known, diamonds. Among the most well-known of Cartier's jeweled masterpieces are the Panther, realized in an array of styles, the Tutti-frutti collection first created in the 1920s, and the St. Petersburg collection that steals one's breath with rubies, emeralds, sapphires and diamonds mixed together in stunning geometrical patterns.

While these companies have entire collections of scintillating timepieces, others offer individual works of wonder. Piaget works magic with its jeweled watch creations, often spending more than a thousand hours crafting a sin-

Left: The "Chatelaine" watch from Van Cleef & Arpels was created in 1990 as a one-of-a-kind. It features pear-shaped, oval and round diamonds set in platinum.

Above: The facade of Van Cleef & Arpels on the Place Vendôme.

Below: Chopard is renowned for its Happy Diamonds series in which loose diamonds float aimlessly as the wrist moves, enhancing their rare beauty and luster. Each watch in this heart-shaped collection features free-moving stones. The yellow-strap model is crafted in 18K white and yellow gold and features 252 yellow and white diamonds on the case; the pink-strap watch is made of 18K white and rose gold, and is set with 252 white an pink diamonds on the case; the blue strap watch is set with 142 diamonds, 110 sapphires on the case.

instance, the ruby is most often referred to as the most precious of all stones, rare and more valuable than top-quality diamonds. This stone is associated with the heart's desires, with love, romance and passion. When coupled in a timepiece with the diamond, which is considered the romantic of all stones (ever since 1477 when Maximilian gave Mary of Burgundy the first diamond engagement ring — forever sealing its fate), a powerful

Above: Known for its animal motifs, Cartier's watch with Dolphins is a masterpiece in ingenuity and elegance. The two dolphins, in their graceful curves, are paved with 1,200 diamonds, weighing more than 32 carats. The ball with which they play is set with more than 22 carats of stones. The master jeweler ingeniously concealed the watch crown.

Above right: Van Cleef & Arpels brings a touch of delicate elegance to this passion-inspired motif. The deep red strap blends beautifully with the 18K gold case that is adorned with 145 diamonds.

Right: Madison Avenue watches. Harry Winston, jeweler to the stars, focuses on the high-society streets of New York City to name its collections.

gle gemstone-adorned bracelet. Other watchmaking greats have their own stunning stories to show. Among them are Audemars Piguet's gemstone dial timepieces that utilize such stones as citrines, amethysts and aquamarine as dials, and the Saratoga Splendour quartet (a unique set of four spectacular gemstone watches) by Concord Watch Company.

Even those Swiss watch companies that do not have entire gemstone lines bedeck at least one or two of their key watch models in diamonds and gemstones. After all, it's difficult to resist the temptation of these dazzling beauties of their earth.

Some watch companies create certain timepieces based on the allure of, or legend behind a particular stone, as each holds a history and myth as rich as its color. For

statement is immediately inferred. The sapphire, too, holds its own lure and has long been the source of many myths. Throughout history, it has been the gem most worn by royalty because of the belief that it offered protection and healing powers. The emerald has also long been credited with mythical powers. The elegant green gem was thought to prevent evil and bring supernatural powers

to the wearer. Timepieces made of these stones typically offer a more mysterious, even mystifying allure.

The adornment of jewels transforms technical wonders into distinctive masterpieces that reflect individual spirit and symbolize the ultimate achievement in jewelry and watchmaking. The creation of high jeweled timepieces is boundless, except for the availability of the stones and imagination of the designer.

Above: From Girard-Perregaux, the Laureato is crafted in 18K white gold and adorned with diamonds and sapphires.

Above left: The emerald, regarded as a gem of tranquility, is the stone of signature choice for the Esmeraude by Concord. Part of the Splendour quartet, this is a one-of-a-kind watch that features moon phase, day, date and month display splendidly ensconced in diamonds and rubies.

Below left: Omega combines emeralds and diamonds on this green strapped work of art.

Below: Rolex adorns some of its key collections with jewels. Shown here is the Oyster Perpetual Cosmograph Daytona watch in diamonds and rubies and diamonds and sapphires.

Secrets of Time

OFTEN, THE MORE we try to navigate time, the more we find it navigates us. That may be the reason why some of the world's top watchmakers try to capture time inside wondrous works of art, elegantly and subtly hiding the watch itself so wearers may have a secret rendezvous with time that is all their own. Over the centuries, as timepieces progressed into pieces of jewelry, art and ultimately everyday necessities, their style and designs similarly transformed. Early portable clocks and watches utilized covers or lids to protect the timepiece. Even when covers were no longer needed to protect watches, new interpretations emerged as art forms, bringing about the rise of today's intriguing "secret" and "hidden" dials on watches. The first notion of "covered" timepieces came in the 15th and 16th centuries. As clocks became more portable, they were set into cases with lids that concealed the clock dial until the owner needed to know the time.

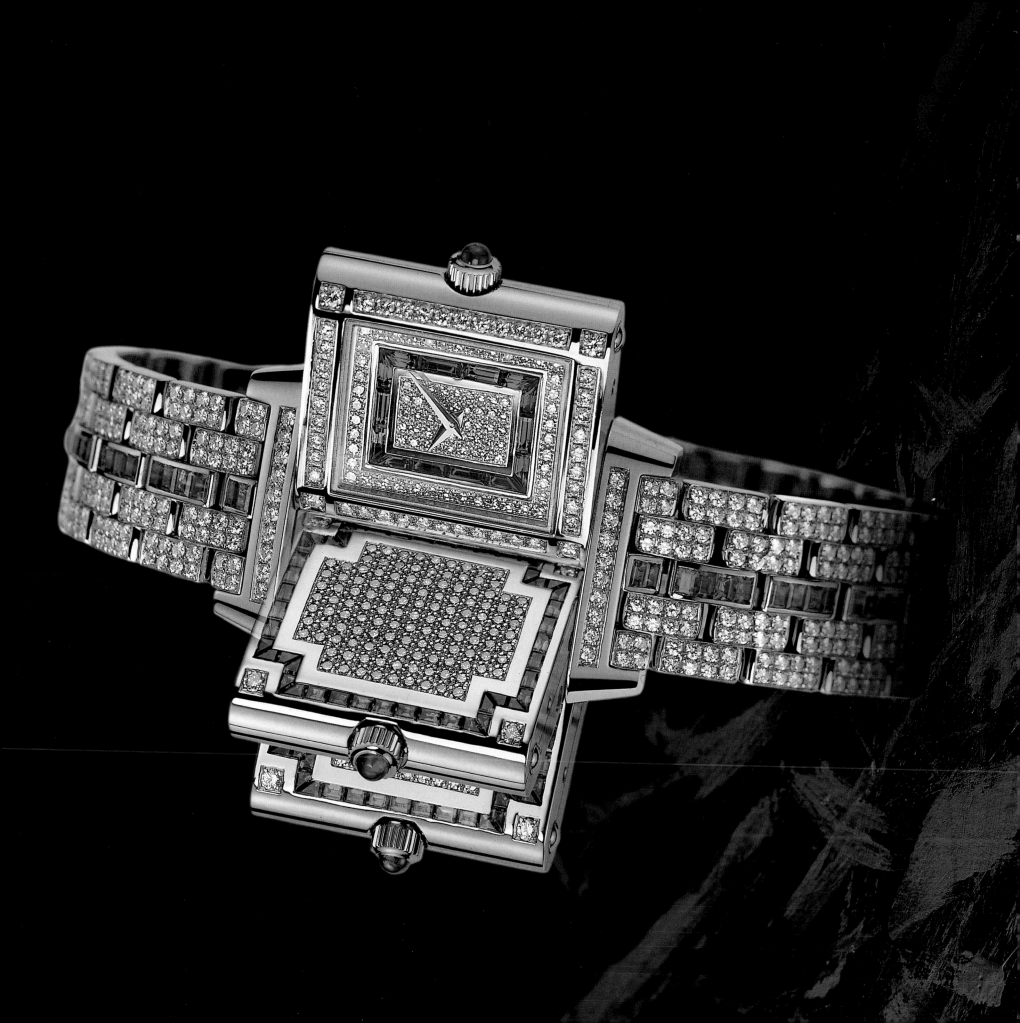

Later, as portable clocks evolved into chate-laines, pendants, fobs and pocket watches, it was necessary to devise a means of pro-tection against rough daily wear-and-tear such as riding horseback, weathering the elements and enduring other treacheries of life in the old days. Covers were still re-quired for practical purposes.

The evolution of this utilitarian case cover to its work-of-art status most likely began during the Renaissance. At this time, as beauty and art became one of the most engaging and exciting parts of life, the tradi-tion of decorating timepieces took a new form.

The earliest means of decorat-ing clock cases was through engraving and etching, and the most popular images were coats of arms, flora, fauna, arabesques, biblical figures and other scenery. Later, these means became more elaborate with the addition of pearls and other gemstones. De-signers also began employing other deco-rative methods such as adding multiple cov-ers, creating par-ticular types of enameling and developing intricately detailed open-worked covers.

Some of the early portable clocks and watches featured multiple covers, including a front cover, a back cover and an inside back cover. One 17th-century timepiece, which is on display in the Musée International d'Horlogerie in La Chaux-de-Fonds, Switzerland, is in the shape of a tulip. It has three petals affixed with hinges that open to reveal the movement. Each side of each petal is decorated with either enamel work or intricate en-graving of bibli-cal figures.

As the art of enamel-ing grew in pop-ularity, new di-rections took hold.

Since, during the 16th and 17th centuries, timepieces were primarily considered a lux-ury — an item enjoyed by royalty or only the very wealthy, it became practice to indulge in self-portraits. It was not unusual for royalty to commission a timepiece with their likeness or the likeness of loved ones painted on the cover, draped

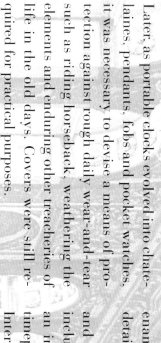

Previous page: Famous for creating the world's first reversible wristwatch, the Reverso, Jaeger-LeCoultre today offers a stunning variety. Page 78: Reverso ring watch from Jaeger-LeCoultre. Page 79: The Reverso Joaillerie reveals the dial on one side and on the other, a gold case set with hundreds of gemstones.

Top and above: Around the 16th century, portable clocks and watches were set into cases with protective lids, which became formats for expression. The rarity of this time-piece comes in its Limoges enamel, unusual for the time. The engraving and piercing work features foliage and strawberry flowers, in a wealth of rich colors from the period.

Top right: The mid-18th century saw a marked interest in the rococo style of decoration which often utilized different shades of gold. This watch by English horologer John Arnold, dates to 1768 and is worked with enamel.

Center: This unusual tulip-shaped watch, from the mid-17th century, features three individual petals with hinges decorated in enamel. The petals open to reveal the move-ment. The tulip-shaped watch was popular in Switzerland around 1625, after the flower was introduced from Holland.

Far left: By the middle of the 19th century, watches were appearing in actual shapes with elaborately decorated covers. These Girard-Perregaux cross-shaped watches date to 1856, while the book-shaped watch is from 1870.

Left: Engraving of animals onto watch cases was one of the most popular thematic designs of the late 19th century. This Tula pocket watch, circa 1894, is crafted in silver and black enamel with a raised gold horse.

Center: In the mid-19th century, the house of Chaumet developed cased watches for royalty. It was Chaumet's style to adorn the watches with enamels and jewels most often pearls, coral, onyx or lapis were used as decoration. These watch case designs were created for Napoleon III and Empress Eugenie.

Bottom left: Frosted crystal, black enamel and diamond brooch watch, called Regence, was created by Chaumet in 1924. When the medallion is turned upward, the watch dial on the other side is revealed.

in the richest hues of emerald green or royal blue.

Enameling of this time was rich and deep. Indicative of the age, most of the enamel work reflected a vibrant reality — scenes and people were accented with gold flanged edges or arabesques, all offering superlative renditions of art.

By the 18th century, English watchmakers were celebrated for their artistry in decorating watch cases with engraved scroll work, garlands, vines and intricate rosettes. Open-worked metal of the most elaborate patterns of leaves and florals became an important design style. In fact, this fine decorative style was inspired by the works of French artists during the reign of Louis XIV, but the English reigned supreme for this type of design known as "piercing."

At the same time, French clock makers were working in a different decorative vein, utilizing a period motif that would come to be known as the "turnip" or also called the French onion. The turnip case is immediately recognizable for its thickness and round shape, much resembling an onion.

The uniqueness of this work was in the decorative cases — most often the watches were covered in leather and painted with gold leaf.

Also in the 18th century the rococo style emerged and that also made its way onto watch cases and covers. This ornamental style often utilized several different colors of gold, combining yellow, white and pink gold and required extensive relief work to achieve depth and dimension.

By the end of the 18th century, this art form gave way to a new, cleaner neoclassical motif. Enamels — especially those

Right: This outstanding timepiece from Van Cleef & Arpels, circa 1941, features faceted sapphires and rubies on each side of a center paved with diamonds, which opens to reveal the watch dial.

Below: Concealed dials on wonderfully sumptuous bracelets is a specialty of Piaget watch company. This timepiece, created in 1950, features a soft mesh bracelet that lifts to reveal the dial.

painted by Genevan artisans — became softer, almost translucent in an effort to offer refined elegance. Gardens and flowers inspired enamelers in ways previously unseen on timepieces.

By the 19th century, all forms of decoration had been utilized, it was but a matter of further perfecting enamel works, colors, jewel setting, and engraving. Pocket watches continued to be adorned with coat-of-arms and other regal dedications, but they were increasingly elaborate. In fact, Chaumet created several beautiful designs for such leaders as Napoleon III, Empress Eugenie and others that featured ornate covers set with diamonds, or accented with onyx, lapis lazuli or coral. Other styles of watch cases and covers also began to emerge. One style featured a tiny watch dial set into an oversized, elegantly decorated case. The dramatic difference in proportion illustrated the tendancy for the aesthetic over the practical.

Also, by the mid-19th century, watches began

emerging in plant and animal shapes. Centuries earlier clock makers had already begun adorning timepieces with ornamental figures such as animals, or mythological creatures to pose as clock-holders or serve as feet for the base of the clock. This practice eventually translated onto watches, as gnomes, gargoyles, Cupids, heraldic lions, dogs and horses were etched into watch case covers.

However, it took until the 19th century for watchmakers to take this incorporation of animals, birds and flowers in watchmaking design a step further — creating actual shapes and discreetly placing

end of technology, art and craftsmanship.

The idea of making a watch with a reversible case was born on horseback. In the 1930s when wristwatches were new and delicate, Polo players continually returned from the field with cracked watch glass. Refusing to part with their timepieces during the game, they asked whether a protective device could cover their watches while they played, and be removed afterward. The request sparked the creation of an enduring delight, the Reverso, which translates to "turn over."

First invented in 1931 in a streamlined art deco format, this watch has withstood the test of time and, more than six decades later, still maintains its noble rank in watchmaking.

The Reverso comes today in many versions and several sizes. In fact, one Reverso housing the caliber 101 movement (the smallest mechanical movement in the world, created by Jaeger-LeCoultre in 1929), remains in the Guinness Book of World Records as the world's smallest watch. But it is not this distinction that makes the Reverso so overwhelmingly intriguing. It is, instead, the artistry of "quick-change" that makes this timepiece special.

The case of the Reverso watch is easily slid in its support and turned completely over, one side revealing a watch dial, the other side revealing a monogrammed gold case back, or — with the current versions — a variety of second dials. The Reverso Florale, for instance, when flipped over, reveals a gemstone adorned rectangle for a jewelry effect, others reveal transparent case backs, monograms, enamel paintings and alternative dials.

Other innovative cover designs of today take their impetus from the past. During the first World War, to protect watches, the dials were often covered with thick metal bars and grids. Today, Cartier has updated this design to cover its Pasha watch.

Above: Known for its Panther timepieces, Cartier's rendition of the Panther realized in this sleek, slinky diamond-adorned watch is not only breathtaking but singularly arresting. In this Taimango Bracelet watch, the Panther lies languidly across the watch dial, which features 1,558 diamonds weighing more than 58 carats, and two pear-shaped emeralds for eyes, as well as an onyx nose.

Top right: Created in 1925, this spectacular jewelry watch in platinum from Omega is set diamonds and a large sapphire adorning the hidden watch dial.

Center: An updated statement in mystery time, this Cartier petal charm watch is smothered in diamonds. The center of the petal charm opens to reveal the watch dial.

Below: Corum's Golden Book series features several different flip-top models. This one, "Love Story," has a cover with a heart-shaped opening. The watch dial is either mother of pearl or 18K gold set with 54 brilliant-cut diamonds.

the watch dial within the form. Typically it was these elegant, artistic pieces of jewelry that took center stage instead of the watch itself.

This concept of fantasy watches was perhaps first fully recognized when a Swiss watch company, Clémence Frères won a silver medal in 1889 for a watch set into a lily-like form decorated in blue enamel and diamonds. The watch dial was set into the center of the flower. It set the stage for a new rendition of luxury watches and these scintillating beauties took the shape of crosses, books, flowers, fruit, animals and insects.

By the turn of the century, watch cases and covers, as well as the watch itself, gained design inspiration from the style and arts of the time. The 20th century ushered in the era of art nou-

veau with stylized ornamentation, then art deco with its geometrics and clean lines, then the larger, bolder retro looks of the 40s and finally, the inception of an "almost-any-thing-goes" look.

As the fine line between watches as utilitarian items and watches as pieces of jewelry became firmly blurred, several wonderful new developments changed the world of the "covered" watch forever. One such advent was the flip-top wrist-watch, in which the wristwatch is created to appear as a jeweled bracelet, but is made with a carefully concealed flip-top that when opened, reveals the watch dial.

This type of wristwatch was created predominantly by the high-jewelry houses and has been a particular favorite of such companies as Cartier, Chanel, Boucheron, Van Cleef & Arpels, Piaget, and Vacheron Constantin. Today, watchmakers delve eagerly into this realm, creating secret watches with elaborate peep-holes or lattice works that offer time undercover.

One of the most significant, breath-taking developments of the 20th century is the invention by Jaeger-LeCoultre of the Reverso, the world's first reversible watch. The story behind this timepiece will go down in the annals of timekeeping as a special leg-

Above: The secret Camellia watch from Chanel is sculpted in white gold and accented with cultured pearls and diamonds for a magnificent floral arrangement.

Center: Ebel's Shanta flip-top watch is an elegant rendition of an open-worked gold cover, adorned with diamonds. Named for the flower of creation in Indian mythology, Shanta was revered as the ideal of womanhood, beautiful beyond imagination.

Below: The Golden Janus from Universal Geneve was first created in 1994. It can be flipped over in the case to reveal a second face that indicates the time in two time zones.

Below left: Lifting out of its case to flip all the way around, this Cabrio watch from Chronoswiss features a watch dial on one side and a sapphire back to reveal the movement on the reverse side.

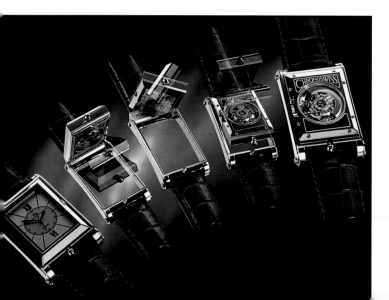

Similarly, other watchmakers use open-worked gold flip-up covers, often adorned with diamonds and elegantly etched gold to create purely beautiful timepieces.

In the early 1900s, advances in shock and water resistancy and the implementation of hardened mineral and sapphire crystals rendered the covers almost obsolete. It was then that covers began to be interpreted on timepieces almost purely for art's sake.

Among the popular themes today in watch covers are designs inspired by books and square-shaped windows. Corum, Van Cleef & Arpels and others have used the book as a medium. In fact, Corum's current book watch opens to reveal not only the watch dial, but also an inscription from a passage in a book. Vacheron Constantin's Jalousie timepiece, first created in 1930 and reintroduced just a few years ago in its Les Historiques line, offers an innovative peek at time. The watch dial is covered by individual strips of gold that, when closed, look like Venetian blinds, but with the press of a lever, the "blinds" open to reveal the watch dial beneath.

Aside from these unusual revealing covers, there are several high-jeweled glories that come to life in timepieces. Masters of this art include Cartier and Piaget, each of which brings passionate beauty and elegance to time. Cartier typifies its heritage in the Panther line, as well as in several other animal watches. Cartier's panthers, created in diamonds and often adorned with sapphires or emeralds, are ingenious works of art and elegance that simultaneously capture the heart and spirit. Piaget masters the elegance of jewels, as well, but focuses on one-of-a-kind masterpieces, such as Blue Passion — a bracelet encrusted in diamonds and sapphires, that opens to reveal a "hidden" watch.

Indeed these jeweled covered works of art are among the most spectacular timepieces of our century. Noted for their ability to allow time to pass by in a secretly seductive manner, these prized possessions have a mysterious hold over watchmakers and watch lovers alike.

Above: One of the most lavish and luxurious hidden watches is Piaget's Blue Passion. This bangle bracelet is set with 572 emerald-cut sapphires and diamonds. The watch cover is set with diamonds and opens on a dial set with 16 trapeze-cut diamonds and a sapphire-set bezel. This exceptional creation holds a total of more than 43 carats of diamonds and more than 93 carats of sapphires.

Center: The poppy flower is a great classical theme of Van Cleef & Arpels that is found in earrings, clips and necklaces.

Left: The serpent is a common element used in jewelry watches. This Bulgari snake is crafted in gold, black enamel, diamonds and rubies with a coiled bracelet of basket-weave gold. Created in 1970, the snake's head lifts to reveal the watch dial.

People in Time

THROUGHOUT THE CENTURIES clocks, watches and wristwatches have been both scorned and coveted, stolen and revered. Their acceptance, advancement and technical progression were often based on the whims of leaders, thinkers and great rulers. Even today, great desire and demand can be stirred for a particular watch or watch brand based strictly on the fact that someone of significance wears it. Indeed, whether that person is a world leader, a financial tycoon, an actor, singer, sports star, or other celebrity, what he or she wears on his or her wrist holds its own influence in time. Beginning with the prominent rulers, leaders, and explorers of the 1800s and moving into today's world of new heights and great personalities, the list of who wears which watch reads like a world's best "who's who." Historically, some of the world's most renowned figures were lovers of timepieces. Among them: Napoleon, Empress Marie-Louise, Marie Antoinette, Queen of France and Empress Josephine.

Previous pages: page 86: U.S. automobile engineer, James Ward Packard (1863-1928) explored the limits of watchmaking technology. This particular watch is the last of 13 watches made for him by Patek Philippe in 1927, and one of the most complicated watches ever made. It features a minute repeater, perpetual calendar, age and phase of the moon, and a rotating 500-star disc showing the night sky above Packard's home in Ohio. Page 87: Patek Phillipe has created timepieces for a number of the world's great people.

Below: Caroline Murat (1782-1839), the sister of Emperor Napoleon the 1st, Queen of Naples from 1808 to 1815, favored Breguet timepieces. Versailles Museum.

Bottom center: The famed British writer and Nobel prize winner Rudyard Kipling (1865-1937) owned this Patek Philippe timepiece, which features a delicate enamel of "Peace Bringing Abundance."

Left: Chaumet designed this watch for the Duchess de Luynes in October of 1853.

Right: The Empress Marie-Louise loved timepieces and jewelry. Painting by Robert Lefevre.

Right center: Cartier served as watchmaker to Duchess Vladimir in 1908.

Early leaders were lovers of several brands. In fact, the houses of Breguet, Chaumet, and Vacheron Constantin played host to Europe's most recognized leaders. Breguet played watchmaker to some of the world's legendary royalty, including Marie Antoinette, Queen of France, Louis XVI, King of France, General Napoleon Bonaparte, Empress Josephine, H. H. Pope Pie VII, Queen Victoria, Sir Winston Churchill and King Farouk of Egypt.

Early explorers also needed timepieces for their expeditions and some of the best stopwatches and time instruments of the 19th and 20th centuries played an important role in history. In 1899, Longines provided five chronometers for an expedition to the North Pole that was led by Louis Amédée de Savoie. Similarly, Roald Amundsen used a Longines watch on his Antarctic expedition in 1911, and Longines watches flew with Admiral Byrd on the fist flight over the South Pole.

The onset of the 20th century saw an influx of great thinkers and leaders, all of whom adored timepieces and recognized their importance in life. C.J. Jung owned an IWC pocket watch (and vicariously through marriage, a portion of IWC itself). Albert Einstein wore a custom-designed Patek Philippe pocket watch. In fact, Patek

Philippe boasts an impressive following, including Queen Victoria, who owned one of the first keyless watches made in 1850, Peter Tchaikovsky, Marie Curie, Rudyard Kipling, Tolstoy, Charlotte Bronte, Admiral Byrd and James Ward Packard.

Other 20th century personality and watch relationships come into play in the realm of politics, space exploration, sports and celebrities in all walks of life. Among some of the key leaders of this century to take to a particular timepiece: former presidents, world leaders and dignitaries.

Corum watches—to be precise, the $20 Double-Eagle Coin watch—are worn by Henry Kissinger, and former presidents Ronald Reagan, George Bush and Richard Nixon.

Jaeger-LeCoultre, in its tradition, has presented an

Atmos clock to some of the world's greatest leaders, either on its own accord, or as an official gift of the Swiss government to visiting dignitaries. Among those who have owned an Atmos: Sir Winston Churchill, Charlie Chaplin, President John F. Kennedy. In the realm of wristwatches, Jaeger-LeCoultre also plays a key role on world leader wrists: Queen Elizabeth II, had a special Jaeger-LeCoultre bracelet watch with the caliber 101 movement created for her coronation. The president of Guatemala wears a 250 TDF by Girard-Perregaux. Jacqueline Kennedy Onassis owned a wonderful jeweled Piaget watch that recently went up for auction (and was bought back by the firm). Her son John F. Kennedy, Jr. has been seen wearing Cartier Tank watch.

In space exploration, several watch brands have played a role. Breitling, Fortis, Bell & Ross and Omega have been on the wrists of top astronauts and cosmonauts, but Omega has perhaps the most elite recognition. It was the Omega Speedmaster watch that went on six Apollo missions to the moon, and was the watch worn by Neil Armstrong when he became the first man to step foot on the moon. What's more,

Top row, left to right: Sir Winston Churchill loved timepieces and is reputed to have owned several. Here he is depicted with a Jaeger-LeCoultre Atmos clock in the background; President Ronald Reagan received a Jaeger-LeCoultre Atmos clock during his term; Harry Winston's Ocean watch is a statement in itself. One was recently seen on the wrist of film star Mel Gibson.

Second row, left to right: Legendary film great Cary Grant shows his Piaget watch to Yves G. Piaget; Queen Elizabeth II wore a Jaeger-LeCoultre watch for her coronation; Actor Rudolf Valentino's character wore Cartier timepieces.

Bottom left: Carl Jung owned an IWC pocket watch with the 24-hour numbers added and his initials CJ monogrammed on the pocket watch case back.

it was the Omega Speedmaster that played a crucial role in saving the lives of the astronauts aboard Apollo XIII.

Certain watches have been spotted on the wrists of top celebrities. Cary Grant wore a Piaget, while Richard Burton was partial to Cartier. Raquel Welch strapped a Breitling on her wrist in the film "Fathom." More current celebrities include Pierce Brosnan, who wore an Omega in the James Bond movie, "Goldeneye." Cindy Crawford wears a specially designed (by her) Omega Constellation watch. Bruce Willis wears a Franck Muller Jump-Hour watch, and Barbara Streisand wears a ladies diamond watch by Franck Muller. Italian actress, Ornella Muti, wears a Chaumet Khésis watch, as does Catherine Deneuve.

Harrison Ford must own a multitude of watches, but he has been seen wearing a Breguet, a Concord and a Breitling. Similarly, Michael Caine has been seen wearing his Breitling Aerospace watch. Elton John, another avid watch collector, owns timepieces by IWC,

Right: In the hit film of its day, "Fathom," movie-queen Raquel Welch strapped a Breitling Co-Pilot to her wrist.

Cartier, Franck Muller and a host of others. Mel Gibson was spotted wearing the Ocean watch by Harry Winston; Dr. Ruth wears a Vacheron Constantin watch; Brook Lee, Miss Universe 1997 wears a Chopard jewelry watch, and fashion designer Giorgio Armani is known to wear either a Jaeger-LeCoultre Reverso or an IWC timepiece. Bruce Springsteen has been seen wearing a Girard-Perregaux Ferrari chronograph.

In terms of movies, numerous watches have starred on the wrists of a variety of stars in great movies internationally. Breitling also co starred on celebrity wrists in the movies, "Independence Day" and

Far left: President John F. Kennedy was given a Jaeger-LeCoultre Atmos clock during his presidency.

Left: While her jeweled Piaget watch was recently up for auction, Jacqueline Kennedy Onassis is seen here wearing a Cartier.

Below left: Ralph Lauren has been seen wearing different watches, but it's clear he enjoys Cartier.

Below: Sylvester Stallone (alongside Arnold Schwarzenegger) wears a Franck Muller timepiece.

Bottom: Pierce Brosnan, in his role as 007, wears an Omega Seamaster in "Tomorrow Never Dies."

"Twister." IWC was in "Air Force One," Franck Muller was a veritable star in "12 Monkeys" as the "12" used in the title is the Franck Muller signature "12" from his timepieces. Jaeger-LeCoultre made a special appearance in "Batman Forever."

Of course, in sports, innumerable connections have been made. Tiger Woods wears a Tiger Tudor by Rolex. Chess great Garry Kasparov wears an Audemars Piguet, while automobile racer Michael Schumacher and Michael Andretti both wear Omega timepieces. Basketball Hall of Fame star, Julius, "Dr. J." Erving wears a Cartier. Golfing great Greg Norman wears an 18-karat gold Chronomat by Breitling. Boris Becker has been seen wearing a TAG-Heuer, and Michael Jordan has been seen wearing an IWC Doppelchronograph, and a Girard-Perregaux Tribute to Ferrari. The list goes on and on. One need only take a good look around to see how celebrities and stars contribute to further promote time.

Blancpain

AT THE DAWN of Swiss watchmaking appears the name of Jehan-Jacques Blancpain, a pioneer who brilliantly perceived his era as one that would shape the history of watchmaking. Jehan-Jacques Blancpain launched the watchmaker's dynasty in 1735 when he set up his workshop in the mountainous Swiss Jura and devoted himself to perfecting the tools that would precisely measure time. Through the generations, craftsmen refined long-standing traditions. To this day, Blancpain holds highest the art of traditional watchmaking — there has never been, nor will there ever be a quartz watch made by Blancpain — yet the watchmaker expertly fuses the expertise built over the centuries with advances in modern technology. Such precise attention to tradition and commitment to excellence make it likely that Jehan-Jacques Blancpain would feel completely at home if he entered Blancpain's modern workshops, today still housed in a farmhouse in Le Brassus, with craftsmen inside who continue to produce hand-crafted timepieces of the highest quality, each displaying time on simplistic round white faces.

Above: Jehan-Jacques Blancpain, founder of the world's oldest watchmaker.

Above: The Carousel of Time, unique in the world, a marvel of art and watchmaking. The carousel houses four pocket watches set with 2989 gems (1645 diamonds, 448 emeralds, 448 rubies and 448 sapphires.) Each pocket watch houses an ultra-slim movement, and is suspended from its own chain. The Carousel itself is comprised of 2.815 kg of white gold, 5059 round diamonds, 12 oval diamonds, emeralds, rubies and sappphires, 192 baguette diamonds, rubies, sapphires and emeralds totalling 200 carats. The creation, worth 10 million Swiss francs, required 10,000 man hours to construct.

Center: Released in honor of Blancpain's 260th anniversary, and the 10th anniversary of the moon phase watch, the new look evokes a link with the 21st century. It's case is slightly larger than the 2100 series model introduced in 1994.

Previous page: The Flyback chronograph. Dedicated to pilots, the chronograph is equipped with the world's slimmest self-winding movement: 308 finely decorated, hand-assembled movements for a height of only 5.4 mm. The screw-in crown, push buttons and caseback guarantee the watch's water-resistance to 100 meters.

Right: Moon phase Watch. The moon phase timepieces provide an eloquent reminder of watchmaking's ancient links to astronomy. First released in 1984. The watch features the smallest self-winding movement displaying the phases of the moon. Far right: Moon phase movement: 261 components, 4.9 mm, power reserve up to 4 days.

The oldest watchbrand in the world was born in the sprawling farmhouse belonging to Jehan-Jacques Blancpain's family. It was typical during the time for craftsmen to work the farms in the summer months, then head indoors during the cold winters to craft watch parts that would be sold in Geneva or Bern. For generations to come, even as the business grew, the Blancpain family continued to produce timepieces from the home-based workshop.

The name Blancpain crossed Switzerland's borders some 30 years after Jehan-Jacques first opened his workshop, when David-Louis Blancpain, the founder's grandson, began taking the timepieces by horseback to sell in France. In 1863, Jules-Emile Blancpain opened the watchmaker's first factory, and immediately began plans to open a larger factory just across the river from the farmhouse. Upon his death in 1928, a Swiss watchmaking journal wrote: "Blancpain is, we assure, the only firm in which management has passed uninterrupted from father to son for more than a century." In homage to its heritage, today's owners hold traditions firm. Jean-Claude Biver and Jacques Piguet, partners who secured the watchmaker just 15 years ago, are reviving the watchmaker with the purest artistic and technological goal: to produce timepieces of perfection featuring the six traditional movements that a watchmaker must achieve in order to become recognized as a master of his trade. This goal has been successfully realized in a little over a decade. Today, Blancpain is considered a leading maker of hand-crafted watches.

A moon phase watch was the first timepiece that Blancpain released under the new leadership, and in testimony to the watchmaker's mission, the wristwatch was the first of its kind: the smallest self-

Left, top and bottom: Typically Blancpain with its sapphire crystal bezel, the Flyback chronograph owes its appeal to the remarkable harmony of its design, it's luminous hands and Arabic numerals of its ebony black dial provide easy legibility in the darkness.

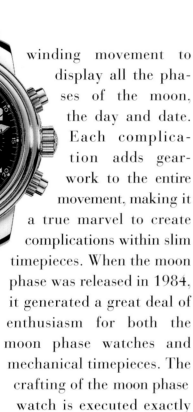

winding movement to display all the phases of the moon, the day and date. Each complication adds gearwork to the entire movement, making it a true marvel to create complications within slim timepieces. When the moon phase was released in 1984, it generated a great deal of enthusiasm for both the moon phase watches and mechanical timepieces. The crafting of the moon phase watch is executed exactly as it has been for hundreds of years. The same craftsmen who hand-polish each part, also engrave the watch's signature number. Blancpain marked its 260th anniversary, and the 10th anniversary of the moon phase watch, with a special version of the celebrated timepiece. Slightly larger in size, it retains the signature simplicity of design for which Blancpain is renowned. The world's slimmest self-winding movement is also found in Blancpain's Flyback chronograph, a tribute to pilots. The flyback mechanism allows the counters of the chronograph to be synchronized by returning to zero, while it is running, and with a push of the button, the chronograph starts again. It's technical features make the timepiece an authentic instrument of navigation, equipped with the world's slimmest movement.

Blancpain's engineers and watchmakers continually advance the development of small-sized complications. In 1988, they released both the slimmest split-seconds chronograph and the smallest minute repeater ever produced, both the product of extensive research. The minute-repeater, the most complicated with its gongs and hammers that strike the hours, quarter-hours and minutes. It takes about 790 hours to produce a single minute repeater wristwatch. But

Left: The Ultra-Slim watch for women. Less than 1.75 mm slim, its slender movement — encased in platinum, yellow gold or stainless steel — demands the full skill and dexterity of the master watchmaker who assembles and polishes it. The hand-sewn leather straps are offered in an array of colors.

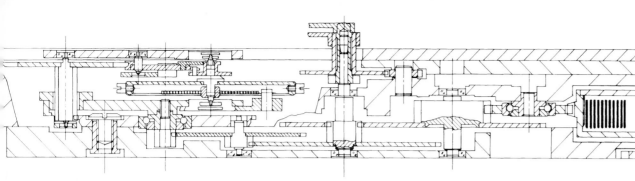

Blancpain adds a exceptional horological artistry. Each caseback features an animation comprised of engraved or enameled scenes, a different scene on each watch.

The ability to develop small movements means Blancpain is one of the only watchmakers to produce complicated masteries for women, as well. It is a practice that began with the watchmaker's craftsmen in 1956, with the release of the smallest movement for ladies' watches called the "Lady Bird." Its smallness granted more freedom for designers to create intricate, elaborate watch faces, without the restraint of bulky, large movements. Blancpain continues to create the "Lady Bird" timepieces, housing the smallest hand-wound movement ever made. The most revered complication, the tourbillon, offsets the affects of gravity, allowing mechanical watches to keep time correctly. In 1988, Blancpain's engineers advanced the mech-anism by developing the first tourbillon with an 8-day power reserve. In 1990, they added another feature, a calendar. The ultimate in complicated watches, a timepiece housing six features, was created in honor of Blancpain's founding year and named the 1735. Introduced in 1991, is it the sum of complications invented during the 260 years the Blancpain has been producingwatches: an ultra-slim movement, moon phase, perpetual calendar, split-seconds chronograph, minute repeater and tourbillon.

Forever forging the generations of experience, Blancpain has released the 2100 watch

Top right: The Ultra-Slim Flyback chronograph.

Above: In 1989, Blancpain marked watchmaking history by introducing the world's first self-winding split-seconds chronograph.

Bottom center: Caliber 1186, self-winding, 361 components, 6.9 mm, power reserve of 40 hours.

— an amalgamation of 21 for the next century and 100 for its 100-hour power reserve. The timepiece is a world first, designed especially with future needs in mind. Perfect for a very active lifestyle, it's face reveals the time even in the dark. The timepiece is also water resistant to 100 meters. In recognition of such forward thinking, the watch was chosen as "Watch of the Year" in 1995/96.

Blancpain's automatic wristwatch is equally impressive as the slimmest of its kind. It is testimony to Blancpain's commitment to producing only the finest timepieces by the most rigorous of standards. With little interest in fashion or trends, the craftsmen are masters of the smallest of details and the essence of the art of watchmaking. The difficulty in creating

these watches is magnified by the deceptively simple white, round face. It's pristine nature allows no room for anything but perfect craftsmanship inside the timepiece, a guaranteethat Blancpain watches will endure as standard-setters for watchmaking for centuries to come.

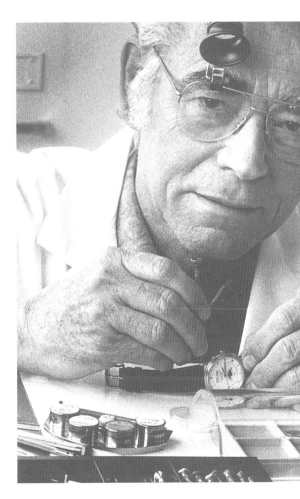

Center, above and below: The Tourbillon watches stand as an example of Blancpain's watch-makers' innovative talent in technology and craftsmanship. In 1988, Blancpain perfected and miniaturised this masterpiece of watchmnaking art and gave the world the first tourbillon with an eight-day power reserve.

Top left: Delicate and complex, the tourbillon is one of the most ingenious mechanical inventions of traditional watchmaking. The mobile carriage of the tourbillon, containing the balance and the escapement, makes on revolution/minute, eliminating performance variations.

Bottom left: Caliber 23, 195 components, 3.5 mm, power reserve of eight days.

Left: A Blancpain master craftsman hard at work.

Breguet

TIMEKEEPING as we know it is owed to the ingenuity and innovations of Abraham-Louis Breguet, an inventor of unparalleled expertise who is regarded as the father of modern watchmaking. From the moment he founded his watchmaking firm in 1775, Breguet's contributions have determined the evolution of the industry. The first automatic watches appeared under his name, known as "perpetuelles." Today's simple watchfaces are remnants of his pursuit of clearly translating time. Once lavishly ornate and overloaded with information, the faces were cleaned up by Breguet, down to the hands that tell the hour. The indicators with hollowed-out points are known as "Breguet hands." But he is perhaps best known for the invention of the tourbillon in 1801. The genius invention counters the effects of gravity and made his timepieces the most accurate in the world. The watchmaker's creations captured the most exacting hearts in history — from Louis XVI of France to Czar Alexander I of Russia to Winston Churchill to modern day collectors and connoisseurs.

Previous page: The wristwatch combining perpetual calendar and perpetual equation of time illustrates the innovative capacity and technical mastery of the Breguet company of today. The only mechanical wristwatch that indicates the equation of time perpetually has been created around a patented movement.

Top: Abraham-Louis Breguet was born in 1747 in Neuchâtel, a thriving and prosperous city where his family had for many years been part of the established bourgeoisie.

Above: Caroline Murat, 1782-1839, sister of Emperor Napoleon, Queen of Naples from 1808 to 1815. Breguet created the first wristwatch ever for her.

Top center: Gold, self-winding "Perpétuelle" pocket watch No 5. Sold to Monsieur le Comte Journiac St Méard, on March 14, 1794.

Right: Sale of a watch to Marie-Antoinette; summary of the sales register (1792).

Below center: Universal self-winding pocket watch with off-centered hour circle, allowing a reading in different time zones. Power-reserve indicator. Silvererd gold dial, hand-engraved on a rose engine. Transparent caseback.

Today, Breguet reigns over the Vallée de Joux, a fertile valley near Geneva, Switzerland where all of the world's most remarkable watches are produced. But his story begins in France, the young Abraham-Louis Breguet left Neuchatel, Switzerland at the age of 15 to study in Paris. His stepfather was immersed in the watch-making business, and the young Breguet naturally took up the craft. Early on, he was recognized as uniquely talented. He was chosen to study under the most accomplished masters in Paris, and after inten-

sive practical and theoretical training, Breguet opened the doors to the shop that would become an institution in 1775. In Paris's center for watchmaking, on the Ile de la Cite, he began refining the masteries of time and developed the first automatic watch, based on years of extensive research, then developed the first gong spring, which rang the hours. At the same time, Abraham-Louis Breguet was designing more elegant, readable watchfaces. Timepieces were crowded with information to be barely legible, the hours were written in Roman numerals and the minutes written in Arabic numerals. Breguet created what no other watchmaker was attempting at the time; highly precise time-telling mechanisms housed in exceptional cases. Such exquisite timepieces enchanted France's aristocracy, and King Louis XVI and Queen Marie Antoinette were fervent admirers. Seduced by watches in neo-classical style and their elegant numerals on enamel or guilloché dials, the ruling couple became dedicated, if

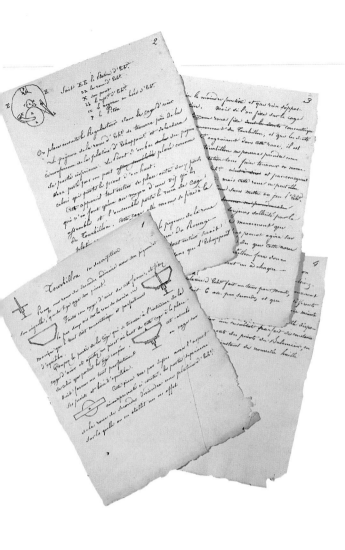

brief, clients. Political turmoil was brewing, and as the French Revolution exploded Breguet returned home to his native Switzerland for two years, where the watchmaker's workshops are located today.

He returned to Paris in 1795 with a wealth of watchmaking revelations swirling in his mind and he quickly fell back into his former habit of catering to France's political elite. Napoleon Bonaparte purchased the world's first carriage clock from Breguet in 1798. In an impressive series of inventions at the twilight of the 18th century, Breguet introduced the "sympathique" clock, which was a system comprised of a clock and a watch. The watch, when placed into a specially designed recess above the clock's face, would be automatically adjusted and reset.

Upper Right: In-line perpetual calendar wristwatch with instant year jump. Patented mechanism.

Above: "Sympathique clock" and its wristwatch, built on the principles developed by A.-L. Breguet in 1793. The watch is automatically set and wound daily when placed into the recess at the top of the clock.

Right: Open-worked skeleton movement with tourbillon and Breguet overcoil balance spring. Hour circle and seconds sector in silvered gold.

It is difficult to name every one of his inventions, but the most important took place in 1801 when Breguet patented his landmark tourbillon regulator. An extremely intricate system, the tourbillon strove to abolish the inaccuracies resulting from gravity or simple movement of the arm. Due to the extremely complicated nature of the system, just 35 examples were produced between 1805 and 1823. The tourbillon, which was honed and perfected throughout the years, is now available in different styles. It is the "tour de force" of the firm's contemporary line.

Abraham-Louis Breguet's delicate touch with watchmaking carried over to a commercial level. He was highly regarded at all European courts and became the watchmaker of reference for the diplomatic, scientific, military and financial elite. He was the Horloger to the French Royal Navy, was inducted into the prestigious Academie des Sciences, and was awarded the Legion d'Honneur by King Louis XVIII. His creations were coveted by dignitaries from all

Above: Men's curved tonneau wristwatch. Self-winding movement; subdial for the seconds. Silvered gold dial, hand-engraved on a rose engine. Water-resistant to 30 meters. Women's version, with diamond bezel, bottom right.

Below: Lady's ultra-slim wristwatch. Bezel and bracelet attachments set with diamonds. Hand-wound movement (1.73 mm). Silvered gold dial, hand-engraved on a rose engine.

Top Left: Lady's self-winding "Marine" watch, with date and center seconds hand. Bezel and attachments set with diamonds. Mother-of-pearl dial, hand-engraved on a rose engine, enhanced with diamond hour markers. Water-resistant to 30 meters.

Left: Intermediate-size "Marine" chronograph. Bezel, strap attachments and clasp set with diamonds. Self-winding movement with date calendar and subdial for the seconds. 30-minute and 12-hour totalizers. Mother-of-pearl dial, hand-engraved on a rose engine. Water-resistant to 30 meters.

corners of the continent. He produced commissioned works for the Sultan of the Ottoman Empire and the Prince-Regent of England. But for Caroline Murat, the Queen of Naples, he offered up a stunning world premiere: an extremely thin watch adorned with a thermometer, which was worn on the wrist.

It is interesting to note that the wristwatch is generally believed to have appeared in prominent circles in the 1880s, and did not usurp the popular pocket watch until the 1930s. Breguet, always considered to be ahead of his time, predicted years in advance that the trend that would capture the globe — he delivered his wristwatch to the Queen of Naples in 1812.

To mark the 250th anniversary of the birth of its founder, Breguet unveiled three exclusive models at the 1997 Basel World Watch, Clock and Jewelry Show. Of breathtaking note, these limited edition models pay tribute to Abraham-Louis Breguet's most important inventions: the self-winding movement, the gong-spring and the tourbillon.

The firm's contemporary collection strives to continue the spirit of cutting-edge innovation begun by its ambitious founder, but it also rests on the shoulders of Breguet's esteemed, technological tradition. Breguet's line of watches can be divided into three main categories: the Classic watches, Marine watches and Type XX chronographs.

Above: Men's self-winding Hora Mundi watch, with indication of the 24 time zones. Winding crown allowing the selection of the desired time-zone setting. Center seconds hand and date calendar. Dial with a special guilloché engraving. Water resistant to 30 meters.

Right: Self-winding "Marine" wristwatch with gold bracelet. Date and center seconds-hand. Silvered gold dial, hand-engraved on a rose engine. Water-resistant to 50 meters.

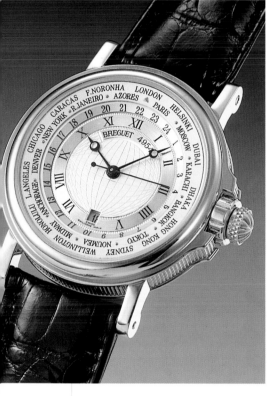

Right: Man's "Marine" chronograph in platinum. Self-winding movement with date calendar and subdial for the seconds. 30-minute and 12-hour totalizers. Silvered gold dial, hand-engraved on a rose engine. Water-resistant to 50 meters.

The Classic line embodies the ideal face of time: clear and precise, they are the celebration of stylistic refinement.

They all faithfully reflect the technical rules and visual principles defined by the company's founder and are best exemplified by the Power Reserve, the collection of Tourbillon watches, the Equation of Time watch, and the in-line perpetual calendar, both patented models.

If there is one field where watchmakers feel the thrill of a challenge, it is undoubtedly in that of "special," often one-of-a-kind models, an area in which the House of Breguet is a past master. The most well-known of these creations, called the "Sympathique" clock was designed by Abraham-Louis Breguet. Now adapted to the wristwatch, this truly amazing "master clock" features a special recess in which a wristwatch is housed to be wound.

The Marine series retains the watchmaking qualities adopted by Breguet when he was commissioned as the Horloger to the French Royal Navy. Their water-resistance and sturdy construction with reinforced case and protected winding-crown mean they can be worn in all circumstances. A recent addition to

the Marine collection is the Hora Mundi model, which displays the time in all 24 time zones, from Hong Kong to Caracas.

Finally, the Type XX chronographs embody the spirit of aviation Breguet harnessed at the turn of the century. Breguet watches were first used by American pilots as early as 1918, and after the second World War, Breguet christened the Type XX chronograph for the French Air Force. As a salute to this cooperation with the aeronautical field, Breguet has created a new generation of Type XX chronographs, which echo all the essential features of the original: the famous "fly-back" function, a robust case, water-resistance to a depth of 100 meters and the rugged style appreciated by the distinguished outdoorsman.

By continuing to uphold for 200 years the tradition of fine watchmaking as defined by A.-L. Breguet, the company has amassed a legacy of inestimable value. Breguet watchmakers are currently exploring the options with a fresh vision, in order to offer their contemporaries modern applications of the traditional arts of measuring time. The result is a collection of very special timepieces that are heavily in demand. Only 7,000 to

The Type XX Aeronavale chronograph with fly-back function. Self-winding movement. 30-minute and 12-hour elapsed-time counters. Small seconds. Graduated rotating bezel. Luminous hands and numerals. Screw-locked crown. Water-resistant to 100 meters. Available in rose gold or steel.

The flyback function. Highly appreciated by pilots, this time-saving device returns the chronograph hand to zero and restarts it immediately – all at a touch of the lower button. Without it three separate actions would be needed to achieve the same result.

Below: Published on Breguet's 250th anniversary, the book "Breguet, Watchmakers Since 1775, The Life and Legacy of Abraham-Louis Breguet (1747-1823)" received wide acclaim as both a reference and an art volume.

8,000 are produced each year. A constant source of inspiration for Breguet's time-pieces is the exceptional archives left by its founder. A rich resource, the archives provided much of the information for the book "Breguet, Watchmakers since 1775, The Life and Legacy of Abraham-Louis Breguet," published on the 250th anniversary, and written by Emmanuel Breguet, a seventh-generation direct descendent, who oversees sales and marketing for the company in France.

Steering the watchmaker today is Jean J. Jacober, Chief Executive Officer of the Groupe Horloger Breguet. The leading watchmaking organization encompasses Montres Breguet, the renowned watchmaking firm that creates the rare and highly prized timepieces; Nouvelle Lemania, manufacturing high-grade mechanical movements for leading watchmakers in Switzerland; and Valdar, a specialized engineering workshop that develops watch components and sophisticated parts for laboratory instruments. All three are based in the Vallée de Joux where the innovations and traditions of Abraham Louis Breguet are upheld by watchmakers who continue to develop top-flight watches based on his founding principles.

BREGUET

HORLOGER DEPUIS 1775

Breitling

SINCE ITS INCEPTION in 1884, the Breitling firm has worked valiantly to define what the perfect watch should be. Many watchmakers devote all their time and energy to aesthetics, creating timepieces whose merits are weighed in polished finishes and exquisitely jeweled faces. While Breitling has never skimped on the importance of an elegant appearance, its watches are not intended to make a high society fashion statement. With their chronograph movements and the amazing circular slide-rule included on the outside bezel of most models, Breitling watches are the epitome of precision. Embraced by pilots since the dawning of aeronautics, the Breitling name is the only one that flies on the wrists of aerobatic aces such as the Blue Angels, the Thunderbirds, the British Red Arrows and the Russian Knights. In fact, Breitling is so synonymous with the air industry that a journalist once mused that "there has never been anyone in a plane's cockpit without a (Breitling) Navitimer on his wrist — or who would at least have wished to have one."

Previous page: Breitling's best-known chronograph is updated with handsome new faces. The Chronomat GT's "instrument panel" dial face features totalizers' with unusual raised frames. The dial features oversized hour markers which, like the hands, are coated with a luminescent compound. Breitling Caliber 13. High-frequency 28,800-v.p.h. self-winding chronograph. 25 jewels. Measures short times to 1/5th second. 30-minute and 12-hour totalizers.

Top: Leon Breitling, the firm's founder.

Right: Gaston Breitling, the heir to the Breitling throne following the death of his father Leon in 1914.

Near right: Gold Chronomat Vitesse. Gaston Breitling worked to perfect Breitling's chronomats, and later went on to patent and market the Vitesse, a stop-watch with a 30-minute indicator and center sweep hand, used by police authorities to trap speed violators.

Far right: A true Breitling classic, the Premier chronograph was first launched in the late 1930s. It was one of the first water-resistant chronographs in volume production. The Premier is now fitted with Breitling's outstanding 43-jewel Caliber 40, one of the most compact watch movements of its kind. Unlike traditional mechanical chronographs, the Premier features a 10-minute and a 3-hour totalizer.

complicated watches, chronographs and the precise measuring tools he invented for the watchmaking industry. When Leon Breitling died in 1914, he passed his innovative baton on to his son, Gaston, who had been meticulously groomed by his father to captain the burgeoning Breitling empire. The company's headquarters had since moved to an expansive complex in La Chaux-de-Fonds, Switzerland.

Gaston dedicated himself to perfecting the company's specialty product, the chronograph, and his Vitesse model was an immediate success.

The future of Breitling was assured on January 26, 1860 when Leon Breitling, intrigued by watchmaking, decided to make it his trade. He had moved to the Swiss Jura from Stuttgart, Germany with his parents, who raised cattle in the summer months and supplemented their winter income by making clock and watch parts. The watch industry was thriving in Switzerland, and out of a total population of 2.5 million people, an estimated 40,000 worked in the industry, producing the intricate mechanisms that made time tick.

The first Breitling studio opened in Saint-Imier, Switzerland in 1884, and the young founder quickly created a niche for his work. He traveled to expositions where he won awards and recognition for his

This design, which was patented and exclusively marketed by the firm, featured a 30-minute indicator and a center sweep hand that intrigued law officials for its ability to efficiently track small increments of time.

Top left: From a technical point of view, the Chrono Jetstream is doubtless Breitling's most interesting chronograph design. Its watchmakers have combined a basic quartz-piloted movement with a fully mechanical chronograph sub-assembly that offers timepiece enthusiasts true mechanical chronograph action and the smooth sweep of a center seconds hand moving at 16 microsteps per second. This exceptional mechanism has an operational life of 4 to 7 years depending on how often the chronograph is actioned.

Top right: The most widely used unit of time, the minute, is the TwinSixty mechanical chronograph's most notable feature. This new Breitling instrument provides two distinct totalizer readouts of the minute. One is located at the center of the dial and runs in tandem with that of the seconds. The other, at 6 o'clock, is a combined two-hand totalizer providing a readout of both hours and minutes.

Below left: The Intruder is equipped with both an analog and an LCD digital time display system, and its standard watch hands show hours, minutes and seconds while its interactive digital readouts facilitate the programming and display of its many other time functions. These include a chronograph, with traditional push pieces and split-time capability, calibrated to 1/100th of a second, an alarm function, a second timezone indicator, civilian or military (12 or 24 hour) option and a time signal.

Below right: Chronomat Longitude

Orders flooded in from police units, and the Vitesse is credited with incriminating the world's first documented speed violators.

With Gaston still at the company's helm, Breitling took the chronograph off its cumbersome chain and moved it out of pockets and onto a person's wrist via a leather strap. Designed as an accent to sportswear, the "wrist watch" captivated military outfits worldwide, and suddenly became an indispensable tool. As industrialization gripped the world before and after World War I, the wrist watch and its timing capabilities held new importance. It became necessary to measure how many revolutions a motor could make in a minute, or how far a vehicle could travel at any given speed. Answering the new demands technology imposed on society, Breitling took the all-calculating slide-rule out of the laboratory and adapted it to the outer bezel of its watches.

Breitling had turned watchmaking into an exacting science. The firm produced what were essentially the first "mini computers," watches that could tell you everything from the time to the answer to number three on your multiplication math test. All of it worked flawlessly, and with the emergence of the aeronautic industry in the early 20th century, the multi-purpose Breitling watches suddenly became a necessity.

In the 1930s, Breitling became the official supplier to the Royal Air Force, and then christened the Chronomat, a watch that boasted a full-fledged logarithmic slide-rule, in 1942.

Pilots clung to them for good reason: besides telling time, the watch was instrumental in calculating air speed, estimated arrival times and even the rate at which their planes consumed fuel.

When Lockheed's 110-passenger Super Constellation took off in 1952 — effectively beginning the age of commercial airlines — Breitling simultaneously introduced its Navitimer, a three-subdial chronograph with an improved slide-rule on the outer bezel (a bezel with talent, as the company likes to say). It catered to the demands of air navigation so well that the AOPA (Aircraft Owners and Pilot's Association) declared the Navitimer its "official watch."

The celebrated Cosmonaute, a version of the Navitimer that still headlines the contemporary Breitling line, earned its fame on May 24, 1962. Perched in a capsule at the top of a simmering rocket at Cape Canaveral, American astronaut Scott Carpenter waited for blast off with a groundbreaking Navitimer strapped to his wrist. The watch (and Carpenter) had to endure being lifted to an altitude of 272 kilometers while experiencing an eight-fold increase in the force of gravity. The watch performed beautifully and then went beyond the call of duty

when a malfunction in the capsule's re-entry equipment forced Carpenter to manually pilot his way home. He used the slide-rule capabilities of his watch to calculate the proper re-entry angle for his pod, and while he splashed down 300 km away from the anticipated spot, he pulled off one of the space program's most heroic rides, making a legend of himself and his timepiece.

Since differentiating between day and night was of no importance to the orbiting astronaut, today's Cosmonaute still features its original 24 (as opposed to 12) hour dial. The Cosmonaute is also the only modern-day Breitling fitted with a hand-wound mechanical movement, exactly like Carpenter's 1962 design.

Breitling's state-of-the-art complex, located in Grenchen, Switzerland, is overseen by Mr. Ernest Schneider. With an expansive line of watches preferred by the distinguished consumer and airmen worldwide, Breitling upholds its motto of producing "instruments for professionals."

Top, left to right: Breitling Rattrapante in platinum; Breitling Rattrapante in 18K gold; Breitling QP in 18K gold.

Bottom: The Montbrillant 1461 is first and foremost a true Navitimer self-winding mechanical chronograph capable of measuring times to 1/5th of a second, featuring a 30-minute and a 12-hour totalizer and equipped with the famed circular slide rule for which this Breitling product line is reputed. The new Montbrillant 1461 chronograph is an alternative design in Breitling's "Grande Complication" product family. Comprising nearly 250 components, its intricately designed movement is programmed to provide a reliably accurate display of the seconds, minutes, hours, day of the week, date, month and phases of the moon over a full 1,461-day period, i.e. during a complete leap-year cycle.

Chaumet
HORLOGERIE

TRACING ITS ROOTS to the glory of the Napoleonic era, Chaumet endures as an inspiring force in the world of innovation and design. The strength imbued by the power of Napoleon's empire launched Chaumet in 1780, when the Emperor selected, among many artisans, Marie-Etienne Nitot to create the imperial jewels for himself, and Empresses Josephine and Marie Louise. It was Nitot who carried out Napoleon's wish that his court should be "beautiful and brilliant," a position of prestige that allowed the House to bear witness to magical moments in history and enjoy access to the spectacular gems held by the court. A talented jeweler and watchmaker, Marie-Etienne Nitot also created the timepieces that Napoleon gave as gifts to his cavalry sergeants, in respect for their protective services. Such suffusion of splendor transcended generations as Chaumet artisans observed the traditions established by Nitot while creating pieces which reflected their times. This set the stage for worldwide recognition as the maker of sleek, modern timepieces.

Today Chaumet is enjoying a renaissance under the leadership of its CEO, Pierre Haquet, supported by its great tradition of craftsmanship and innovation, handed down from previous generations. Now with international presence, the jeweler's luxury timepieces stand on their own — even as they harmonize with Chaumet's line of Nouvelle Joaillerie — and are sure to outlive passing trends.

In a sign of the times, Chaumet's most recent collection of watches, "Style de Chaumet" captures the idyllic blending of romance and elegance, a fusing of sleek lines in a bold design. Strong lines of gold encase round, square or rectangular watchfaces, in large or small timepieces. Chaumet takes this elegance and updates it with the use of stainless steel as well as gold, and in a fanciful twist, adds a patent leather band. For a more striking contrast, Chaumet adorns a stainless steel bezel with a gold band, edged with stainless steel.

The custom feeling of the watch is enhanced by a variety of watchfaces, in rose, blue, gray or white, some luxurious with diamond indicators, others with tone-on-tone designs. The possibilities are numerous... the "Style de Chaumet" comes in more than 70 variations, all in eye-catching designs, all pure in form, the collection is the epitome of C h a u m e t style.

T h e difficulty is in choosing: will it be the newer square shaped bezel with a gold band, or the round silver-red dial circled in steel with a leather strap, or a rec-

Previous page: Style de Chaumet watch, small rectangular model with diamonds

Above: Large rectangular Style de Chaumet watches in yellow gold with white dial and Roman numerals or diamond indexes, on a yellow gold bracelet. Two sizes.

Above right: Large yellow gold rectangular Style de Chaumet watch, white dial, quartz movement. Large yellow gold round Style de Chaumet watch, white dial, automatic movement. Both with crocodile bands.

Right: Style de Chaumet watches, large steel square model and large steel round model.

or the Paris-Dakar Rally are immediately brought to mind with a glance at the chronograph. With its classic workmanship, the watch radiates the fluid lines of modern geometry... Yet there is the impression that it ranks among the great classics.

The chronograph is available in either quartz or automatic, with a Piguet 1185 movement, with straps, assuring Chaumet's presence in the world of technical watches.

In reverence to the universe's most magnificent star, Chaumet names its most popular watch Khésis, the Native American word for sun. Distinctly feminine, the Khésis watches are complemented by a coordinating line of "Nouvelle Joaillerie."

The Khésis line exudes the same warmth, sophistication and beauty as Inès Sastre, the "Face of Chaumet." The 23-year-old model and actress embodies the energetic elegance of Chaumet's line of timepieces. Adorning the wrist are a series of supple links, in the shapes of rice in either gold or steel,

Left: The 18K yellow gold self-winding movement chronograph on leather strap

Below: The steel chronograph on leather strap, quartz movement

tangular mother of pearl dial, its bezel covered in a glorious diamond pavé on a taffeta strap. No matter what the choice, each watch is thoroughly contemporary yet evokes deep association with France's glorious past, its style reflecting a great tradition of aesthetics and craftsmanship.

One of the newest additions to the Style de Chaumet line is the Chronograph, which features the same sleek design and pure lines, but interpreted through a more rugged, sporty approach. In either steel or gold, with a black dial, its sturdy bezel perfectly reflects current stylish trends.

The Monte Carlo Formula One race,

Above: The white gold "Khésis Top Lady" watch and the yellow gold "Khésis Classic Lady" watch. The center of the dial is set with diamonds for both models.

Right: Steel Khésis Top Lady with gray dial. Steel Khésis Classic Lady with diamond bezel. Steel Khésis Top Lady, with a black dial and diamond indexes.

creating a textured, flexible bracelet that is comfortable for every occasion. In either all gold or all steel, the stunning timepiece is made more precious with the addition of pavé diamonds on the bezel, then raised to another level of luxury when the pavé diamonds spread outward, coating the bracelet.

The watchface ranges from bold, Roman numerals to diamonds or sapphires marking the hour, to a face sprayed in diamonds, reflecting the time and the eternity of the world's most precious gem in blissful harmony.

At once ultra-modern and then refined, it is the timepiece for the contemporary woman, whether she is a "Top Lady" desiring the larger sized version, or a "Classic Lady," favoring the smaller dial.

To heighten the luxury of the moment, a woman can wear a Khésis necklace, bracelets and rings, creating a stunning ensemble that is sure to captivate. The Khésis jewelry collection echoes the motif of the watch bracelet, in all its luxurious variations, including the pavé diamond version. By layering the pieces, a woman retains the option to change at a whim, for a more toned-down approach, perhaps just the

watch and a bracelet, or wearing the Khésis necklace, ring, two bracelets and diamond pavé timepiece, for an evening out. It is the perfect ensemble for the contemporary woman who enjoys the ease of today's fashion, but aspires to the exquisite luxuriousness at a moments notice, that the complete Khésis collection can bestow.

Artisans of exceptional talent work with the most precious of materials to create such magical timepieces. It's all in the tradition of Joseph Chaumet, the third generation leader who gave his name to the jeweler and in 1907 moved to its present quarters at 12 Place Vendôme. It was also Joseph Chaumet who moved all of his craftsmen under one roof at the Place Vendôme address, where he would supervise the creation of every piece, from conception to the

Left: Inès Sastre is wearing watch and jewels from the Khésis collection. All yellow gold.

Below from left to right: Gold Khésis Top Lady watch with a white dial and diamond bezel and indexes. Gold Khésis Top Lady watch with pavé diamond dial, bezels and three motifs of the bracelet. Gold Khésis Classic Lady watch with gold dial and pavé diamond center. Gold Khésis Classic Lady watch, white dial.

final polishing, a standard that continues today.

Chaumet's versatility, a fusion of simplicity and elegance, is evidence that the House is carrying on the dream started by its founder, Marie-Etienne Nitot. It was he who first attracted the attention of great minds... and established Chaumet's tradition of creating wearable, elegant items, evoking the spirit of the times.

Chopard

To SOME, it may come as a surprise that one of the most enduring companies in watchmaking — one that for years has been producing some of the most beautiful jeweled watches in the world — has only recently crafted its own movement. But by doing so, the House of Chopard is fully realizing dreams that began two generations ago. Joining the ranks of an elite group of watchmakers, Chopard is now undergoing production of its automatic calibre L.U.C. 1/96, which is first appearing in the men's watch called L.U.C. 1860, named in honor of the company's founder, Louis Ulysse Chopard. Several years of covert planning surrounded the development of the new movement and, as owner Karl-Friedrich Scheufele recalls, the tedious process advanced with few results, causing Chopard executives to frequently consider dropping the idea.

Previous page: The L.U.C. watch (bottom). Men's watch housing the new L.U.C. 1.96 movement, in 18K white gold with copper-plated guilloché dial. At top, the men's watch housing the new L.U.C. 3.96 movement, in 18K gold with white dial and gold hour-markers.

Above: The Scheufele family, from left: Karl-Friedrich, Caroline, Karin and Karl Scheufele.

Far right: "Tonneau" with perpetual calendar in 18K yellow gold, automatic movement, indications of the phases of the moon, date, days of the week, month and leap-year, silvered dial.

Below: Classical men's watch in 18K yellow gold with double-going barrel, automatic movement, power reserve, permanent small seconds hand.

Left: The 18K gold "Tonneau Réserve de Marche." Its case, water resistant to 30 meters, houses an automatic movement with a power reserve indicated at 3. Its elegant face displays a silver guilloché dial, with applied gold roman numerals.

With just months left under Chopard's original deadline a new team began redesigning the automatic calibre. They triumphantly emerged in January of 1996 with a movement that pleased the entire board at Chopard, and more importantly, with a piece that signals the direction of the company for years to come.

In a proud display of craftsmanship, the L.U.C. 1860 is being produced with transparent backs in a limited edition release of 1.860 watches, in 18K yellow gold, white gold or rose gold. A resolutely modern timepiece housed in Chopard's Classic style, its designers sought to highlight, through pure lines, the excellent quality of the movement. Water resistant to 30 meters, the watches slightly domed sapphire crystal and lugs are perfectly fitted to the wrist.

The timepiece carries forth the prestige of the "Manufacture" stamp, a Swiss designation reserved for products that have been hand-made, every step of the way. Indeed, more than 130 years ago, Louis Ulysse Chopard was renowned as expert in the production of the calibres during his time. His reputation earned him the line as main supplier of the legendary Swiss railways. And it was his reputation that originally drew the Scheufele family to buy the company.

In 1860, Louis Ulysse Chopard set up shop and declared that he would be producing the best precision watches in Sonvilier, Switzerland. The proclamation was echoed by scores of other prestigious watchmakers on the Swiss mountainsides. The industry buzzed with incessant developments: from the invention of the crown

winder to the development of affordable watches to the first mass production.

The excitement endured until the Turn of the Century, when the Industrial Revolution brought factories and mass production to Switzerland, crushing the cottage industry. Instead of closing up shop, a determined Louis Ulysse Chopard packed up his watches and set out to find new clients by venturing east: to Poland, Hungary and the Baltic States and Russia. When he returned, his cases were empty and his new client list included Czar Nicholas II. Inspired by the success, Louis Ulysse Chopard moved his shops to Geneva where he knew he would attract international customers. Despite two world wars, he and his sons prospered for the

next four decades.

Yet by 1963, the passion for watchmaking had withered from the family bloodline and Chopard's grandson, Paul André, was left with a heart wrenching dilemma. Already in his 80s, he could no longer run the business and both of his sons were pursuing professions outside of the family tradition. He knew he would have to find a buyer. After many sleepless nights, relief came. Karl Scheufele visited the Chopard factory and announced that he was interested in the company.

Both businesses share a certain symmetry: Scheufele's grandfather founded his own jewelry and watchmaking company in 1904 and had traveled to the other side of the world (the United States) at the same time Paul André Chopard's grandfather made his successful business trip to Eastern Europe. In 1963, the companies were making major decisions at the same time. Just as Chopard had decided to sell the business, Scheufele was looking to buy its own watchmaking company in order to liberate the company's reliance upon external sources.

Happy to strike the deal, the Scheufele

Above: Automatic chronograph in 18K yellow gold, water-resistant up to 100 meters, minute and hour-counters, date, screwed-down crown, gold hour-markers, luminous points.

Top left: L.U.C. plate, pricelist, sketches of pocket watches.

Left: Happy Diamonds collection in 18K yellow gold with five free moving diamonds, pink leather band.

Far left: Happy Diamonds collection in 18K yellow gold with seven free moving diamonds.

family immediately began expanding the company, with an eye on the future and a strong foothold in the past. Karl Scheufele and his wife, Karin, ran all of the operations and the couple later moved to larger quarters in Meyrin, just outside of Geneva in 1974. The couple runs Chopard — as well as the production in Pforzheim, and now its new movement manufacture in Fleurier — along with their children, Caroline Gruosi-Scheufele and Karl-Friedrich Scheufele, both of whom are vice-presidents. To this day, Chopard's self-reliance is preserved by retaining experts at every level of production: goldsmiths, polishers, stone grinders, engineers, casters, designers, etc. The list

is endless, and costly. But Karl Scheufele explains that this system allows Chopard its flexibility to both compete in changing markets and cater to any inspiration.

In testimony to Scheufele's philosophy, Chopard now produces 30,000 watches and 15,000 pieces of jewelry a year, as compared to only a few hundred pieces just over 25 years ago. Both lines are distributed through the companies subsidiaries in France, Germany, Italy, Austria, Spain, Russia, Singapore and the United States, and collectors can find the watch or jewelry of their dreams in exclusive boutiques all over the world, from Geneva to Athens, Baden-Baden, London, Paris, Vienna, New York, Dubai, Hong Kong, Jakarta, Kuala

Lampur, Osaka, Singapore, Taipei, Tokyo and most recently, Moscow, Mumbai, Istanbul, Kuwait and Cannes.

The pursuit of the "Happy Diamonds," a watch based on one designer's fascination with waterfalls, is one inspiration that tested the limits of Chopard's engineers. Fresh from a visit to the Black Forest, upstart watch designer Ronald Kurowski sketched plans for a watch in which several diamonds would cascade freely across the watch face, much like a waterfall he saw in the woods.

"Brilliants first reveal their beauty and their fire when they move. That's why I have always been angered by the way in which mountings severely restrict the movement of the stones. My watch will finally change all that." The sketches were immediately chosen as the most interesting design of the year and entered in competition for the prestigious "Golden Rose" of Baden-Baden. The watch would have to be ready in three months.

What Kurowski — a newcomer to the industry — couldn't have anticipated were the design challenges that his ideas posed. By allowing diamonds, the hardest surface in the world, to roll freely within a watch casing he created one of the most problematic tasks: glass would be scratched in no time. What material could Chopard use to house the brilliants? How could they stop the diamonds from turning over to reveal their backs?

Gold, painstakingly applied in thin sheaths on the back of each brilliant kept the diamonds from scratching the watch crystal. Happy Diamonds is the most renowned and successful timepiece Chopard has created and it has inspired scores of other pieces, including the jewelry line launched by Caroline Gruosi-Scheufele.

Launching a sport's watch line was a drop in the bucket, literally, for Karl-Friedrich Scheufele, who oversees Chopard's line of men's watches. During a visit to Hong Kong in 1980, he dropped the St. Moritz sports watch into a champagne ice bucket in a daring test of the watches waterproof ability. Although the watch was still undergoing testing, Karl-Friedrich Scheufele took the risk because his cus-

Far left: The Chopard Museum in Geneva

Left: Chronograph in steel with mechanical movement, indication of one-fifth of a second, minute and hour-counters, sapphire crystal case-back, dark grey dial.

Below: St. Moritz collection: men's watch in stainless steel, automatic movement.

1000 MIGLIA ›

Above right: the 1997 Mille Miglia watch, specially produced for the 70th anniversary of the race, this watch is a chronograph fitted with a self-winding movement. In steel with date display, tachometer, minute and hour-counters.

In its present form, the "Mille Miglia," as a race between classic vintage automobiles, has taken place every year since 1977 in northern and central Italy. In 1988 Karl-Friedrich Scheufele, under the Chopard name, decided to become the main sponsor of the resurrected and now extremely popular event.

Below: Mille Miglia collection: ladies watch in gold/steel, set with 16 brilliants and 8 sapphires, chronograph, water-resistant

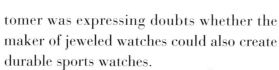

tomer was expressing doubts whether the maker of jeweled watches could also create durable sports watches.

"I had no idea if the watch would actually survive such treatment," Karl-Friedrich Scheufele says, recalling that the incident happened at a time when water-proof watches were still in their infancy. Two anxious hours later, the watch was fished out, yet it was running just as it was before it took the plunge. That incident proved that the junior member of the family had astute business sense — and the St. Moritz line was heralded as "the pioneer." Since then, the watch has become one of the most sold sports watches in the world, labeled by critics as sporting, masculine, very chic and very expensive. Chopard's line

of sports watches has been expanded to include the "Monte Carlo" and, in 1986, the more feminine "Gstaad" collection designed by Caroline Gruosi-Scheufele.

For ten years, Chopard has also celebrated the classic "Mille Miglia" race with its own watch of the same name. And each year, Chopard presents the participants with the latest "Mille Miglia" watch, each case-back engraved with the individual's starting number. The 70th edition time-piece marks a premier for the "Mille Miglia" line because it is the first time the chronograph has been fitted with a self-winding movement.

Time-honored classics are beautifully crafted by Chopard's designers. The elegant tonneau watch, enriched with complications that include a retrograde perpetual calendar, displays on its face the date, the month, the year and the phases of the moon. It takes more than a month to craft the 326 parts of the calendar, and proud to

ing in the L.U.C. 1860 timepiece, Chopard now controls every step along the way toward creating and developing its timepieces. From the breathtaking craftsmanship of "Happy Diamonds" to the cutting edge of its Sports Watches to the development of its own movement, Chopard continues to demonstrate its leadership and commitment to developing the most elegant and sophisticated watches in the world.

Left: Perpetual calendar chronograph in platinum, automatic movement, 24-hour register, indications of the day, date, week, month, leap year, seasons and phases of the moon.

Below: Lady's watch in 18K yellow gold set with 36 diamonds. Available in polished yellow gold.

show it off, the artists expose their work through an elegant skeleton movement. Among Chopard's most highly celebrated men's watches is the perpetual calendar chronograph. A "chef d'oeuvre," comprised of 478 individually hand-polished components, the timepiece took over a year to develop. The watchface displays the date, month, year and the moon phase, while the bezel is edged with a tachymetric scale. In a limited issue of three numbered series of 50 in platinum, yellow gold and rose gold.

And now, Chopard has achieved the final phase of self-sufficiency. With the development of its own movement, premier-

Concord

CONCORD IS RENOWNED for creating timepieces of exceptional design and innovative technology — a perfect concord of form and function. The company was founded in 1908 in Bienne, Switzerland, by two young watchmakers who sought to develop extremely thin movements that would allow them to realize timepieces of beautiful proportions. By 1915, some of the world's most elite jewelry houses recognized Concord's excellence in engineering and design, and commissioned the young firm to make their luxury watch lines. Over time, the advanced technology pioneered by Concord has yielded timepieces that have been popular with succeeding generations, as well as watches worthy of the realm of Haute Horlogerie. The firm's early achievements were a harbinger of exciting developments to come. In 1979, Concord stunned the industry with Delirium, the thinnest watch ever created. Since then, Concord has unveiled magnificently jeweled, highly complicated, one-of-a-kind marvels, some featuring unprecedented technology. Approaching its first century mark, Concord unquestionably affirms the noble aspirations of harmony and symmetry implicit in its name.

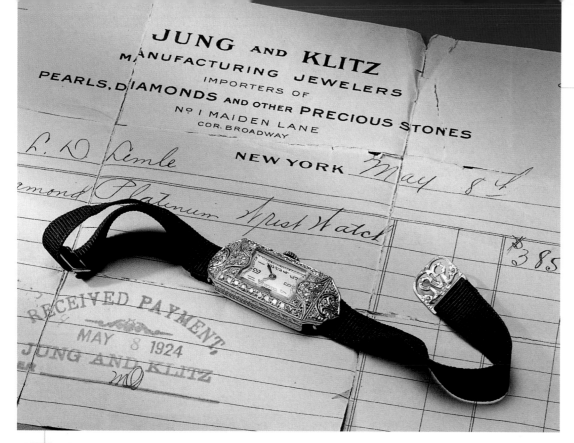

Below: Two views of Delirium. One shows the paper-thin platinum case and dial. The other is a skeleton dial with diamonds and an 18K gold case and diamond bezel.

Bottom: Concord Watch Co. pioneered and perfected the ultra-flat quartz movement that enabled the creation of extremely thin watches. Here, the Delirium is pictured on a compact disc to illustrate its extraordinary thinness.

industry: "the thinnest watch in the world."

The first generation Delirium achieved a minuscule thickness of just 1.98 millimeters, dimensions accomplished by the fact that the movement itself was constructed as part of the case back. The Delirium evolved quickly, and Concord's craftsmen issued a Delirium II later the same year. A technological marvel, the second Delirium

Previous page: Rubeus. The vivid beauty of autumn is captured in this timepiece. The bezel features 38 diamonds of over 9.30 carats and eight rubies totaling 2.40 carats. The dial features 24 baguette rubies and 288 pavé diamonds.

Top: Early Concord dress watch. This elegant platinum and diamond ladies' watch sold in 1924 for $385, according to the information on the jeweler's receipt.

Above: Concord eight-day clock, one of Concord's most popular products. Presidents Calvin Coolidge and Harry S. Truman owned them and frequently gave them as gifts.

In the 1920s, Concord accentuated its watchmaking prowess by becoming an innovator in clock design. They introduced the legendary Ring Clock, a soon popular travel alarm clock. A ring attached to the case served as a stand. President Harry S. Truman, seduced by the clock's elegance and functional design, made it into a favored diplomatic gift: he honored the heads of state present at the Potsdam Peace Conference by offering each a Concord Ring Clock.

A true pioneer in the evolution of the wristwatch, Concord defined what the fashionable wrist-worn timepiece should be. The Swiss firm inspired elegance with innovative new designs that included medallion wristwatches, watches with lids, and the stunning covered-bracelet watch of the 1950s — today a highly coveted collector's item.

Concord reached a distinguished pinnacle in watchmaking history when it introduced the Delirium watch on February 12, 1979, a timepiece that finally lay claim to the most sought-after appellation in the

broke the 1.5 millimeter barrier, only to be bested by a 1981 version that measured an astoundingly thin .98 millimeters.

Delirium models that grace Concord's contemporary line are still unsurpassed in thinness: those heirs to the nearly 20-year-old original with caliber 20 or 90 movements feature cases thin to a point of less than three millimeters; their quartz movements only .98 millimeters thick. Their trademark rectangular cases are exquisitely crafted of the finest 18K gold, stainless steel or steel and gold.

Linking the elite worlds of watchmaking and Haute Joaillerie, Concord has punctuated the last few years with incredible masterworks such as the Saratoga Exor. "This one-of-a-kind creation stands alone as the ultimate Saratoga watch," said Gedalio Grinberg, the Chairman of Concord Watch Company, at the Exor's unveiling on April 26, 1995. "It is the most sophisticated timepiece in a line of watches known for its perfect balance of Swiss craftsmanship and elegance."

The watch boasted a complicated tourbillon mechanism, and its exterior, carved from a custom alloyed platinum bar weighing 700 grams, was embellished with

Bottom right: Mariner V Centenario Collection: Five one-of-a-kind timepieces of extremely complicated and even unprecedented technological innovation.

Above: La Scala detail. The geometric case, bezel, bracelet links and radiant diamond accents of the rich 18K gold ladies' La Scala watch create a statement in contemporary elegance. This close-up photograph illustrates the brilliant diamond bezel, bracelet accents and hour markers, as well as the unique clamshell design of the dial.

Right: La Scala (bracelet pair): The angular grace of the 18K gold La Scala derives from its bold bracelet – each link carved, not stamped, from a solid block of gold – the square, polished bezel, and unique wave-patterned dial. The ladies' model has diamond accents and diamond hour markers.

118 flawless D color diamonds. Finally, the watch's spectacular movement was showcased via a sapphire dial, crystal and caseback that were completely transparent. The Exor was breathtaking at its unveiling, and is likely the most expensive wristwatch ever sold: it was purchased by a distinguished collector for two million Swiss francs.

While there is only one Saratoga Exor in existence, the original Saratoga design first appeared in 1986 as the flagship of the Concord line, a luxury watch easily accessible to the world market. To celebrate the 10th anniversary of the birth of the Saratoga, Concord issued an updated version of the watch in 1996 and christened it the Saratoga SL series.

The SL stands for "Sport Luxury," and the series is defined by an athletic, styl-

ized design, which complements the modern-day climate of casual elegance and responds to the demand for a versatile watch that suits an active lifestyle. Available in a myriad of styles, the essential SL model is a sporty stainless steel and 18K gold design with bracelet or strap. For consumers looking for the utmost in elegance, the watch can also be delivered in solid 18K gold, set with diamonds and elaborate dial.

In conjunction with the launching of the Saratoga SL line, Concord also released its Veneto collection in the early months of 1996. Primed to counterbalance the sporty

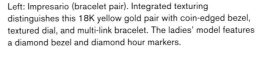

Left: Impresario (bracelet pair). Integrated texturing distinguishes this 18K yellow gold pair with coin-edged bezel, textured dial, and multi-link bracelet. The ladies' model features a diamond bezel and diamond hour markers.

Bottom center: Concord Impresario Limited Edition Certified Chronometer in rose gold has an automatic movement with 72-hour power reserve.

is the epitome of traditional opulence.

Always exploring new ways to combine the technical mastery of watchmaking with the ornate lavishness of high-society jewelry, Concord unleashed an unprecedented quartet of one-of-a-kind watches to inaugurate the 1997 season. In honor of the 25th Basel Watch, Clock and Jewelry Fair, Concord exhibited its Saratoga Splendours series on April 10 of that year. The collection, which has an aggregate value of three million Swiss francs, pays homage to the four cardinal gems of the world: the ruby, emerald, sapphire and diamond.

Each unique timepiece showcases a different gem and features a platinum case and crown set with a specially cut diamond, crocodile leather strap and feuille hands. The set, which took over a year to produce, reveres the mythic powers humans have associated with gemstones for centuries. A stunning collection, the Saratoga Splendours is the watchmakers' latest offering, and a perfect marriage of beauty and technology from Concord.

aura of the SL line, Veneto was an expression of pure elegance, inspired by the lush landscape and architectural wonders of the Veneto region of Italy. The 18K white or yellow gold bracelet is made up of alternating rectangular and curved links, each individually polished to enhance the rich glow of gold. The exquisitely crafted Veneto collection offers the choice of a round, rectangular or banana-shaped case, optionally embellished by radiant, fully-cut diamonds. Concord's Veneto

Saratoga Splendours Collection:
Top: Adamas. The symbol of winter with a 46-diamond bezel totaling 10.50 carats. The dial is distinguished by 199 pavé diamonds and is set with 26 baguette diamonds.

Above: Esmeraude. The bezel is set with 38 flawless diamonds and eight trapezoid-shape emeralds, the gemstone of the spring. The dial features 279 pavé diamonds and is set with 12 baguette emeralds on hour indication and 24 baguette emeralds adorning a day and date perpetual calendar.

Franck Muller

"THE FIRST TIME EVER" is a tough claim to achieve once for any inventor, let alone on a routine basis. But since the mid-80s, that is exactly what Franck Muller has done with his remarkable timepieces. The seemingly unstoppable innovator has 21 world premiers and four patents to his name, all developed over the past 10 years. The latest creation? Muller has, for the first time, incorporated the bell chimes — once reserved only for the pocket watch — into the wristwatch. When the bells chime on the Calibre 97, they are not only sounding the hour, they are signaling another great moment in watchmaking created by one of the youngest creators in the industry. Franck Muller's enthusiasm for his craft — and the onslaught of rapid-fire changes he is perpetuating within the watchmaking industry — is sparking new generations of collectors. He's drawn fans, from royalty, to presidents, to stars in the entertainment industry and, of course, long-time watch collectors, simply by mastering the construction of complications (features that enable a watch to keep precision timing or do more than tell the time, such as a lunar dial) while still designing the most eye-catching watches in the world.

Previous page: 1992 WORLD PREMIERE The most complicated wristwatch in the world. This unique piece makes an extraordinary mark in the world of Haute Horologe. Never before has such a complicated wristwatch been created: Grande and petite sonnerie, minute repeater, a perpetual calendar programmed up to the year 2100 with date, day of the week, month and monthly retrograde equation, cycle of leap years, 24-hour indication, moon phases, indication of internal temperature of the mechanism. The movement is contained in an Empire-style watchcase, made from a block of 950 platinum. In 1995, a Tourbillon was added.

Above: 2852 T (Imperial Tourbillon) Mechanical watch with manual winding , visible Tourbillon, small second counter, case in solid yellow 18K gold, water-resistant up to 25 meters.

Franck Muller in his workshop at the Chateau in Genthod.

It wasn't always evident that Franck Muller would become a visionary creator of time-pieces. He wasn't born into an enduring house of watchmaking and he seemed to lack direction early on. Leaving high school at an early age, he could be found wandering around flea markets, a pastime he enjoyed since he was a child. Muller says he often browsed the markets in search of antiques when one day a friend noticed his interest and patience in taking objects apart. Muller's friend advised him to study the repair of watches, a craft that sorely needed experts at the time. This ultimately led Muller to the Ecole d'Horlogerie of Geneva, where he found his life's work. "My school experience in Geneva was fantastic because I had found exactly what I wanted

to do," Muller says. "I had tried different jobs in my young career, mosaic work, cabinet making, mechanical engineer, and many others, for which I had the inclination." But for Muller, "watchmaking is the perfect union between art and technique."

One anecdote that is often retold is the story of what Franck Muller did with the Rolex Oyster he received for graduation. Instead of proudly wearing it on his wrist, Muller took it apart and added a retrograde perpetual calendar of his own invention. "The Rolex seemed simple to me, and I find it interesting to add other functions," Muller explains. He began the prestigious task of restoring timepieces, mostly pocket-watches, for auction houses, and he began to notice that the advancement of complications in

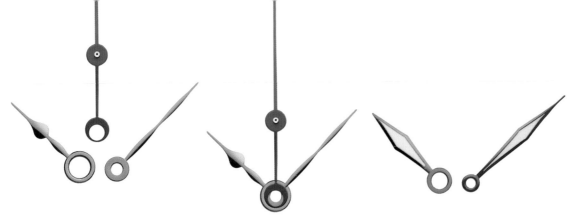

hand-crafted wristwatches had stalled, most certainly because such work would mean scaling down to pinpoint miniaturization, a tedious challenge. Soon afterward, he began revolutionizing the watchmaking industry through his developments of complications.

The first challenge he undertook was perhaps the most difficult: the Tourbillon complication. The complex mechanism that eliminates errors occurring naturally due to the pull of gravity had seen few advancements since it was invented by Abraham Louis Breguet in 1801. In 1986 Muller became the first person in 175 years to get a new patent for his tourbillon watch. What's more, the patent encompasses both the progress in technology and the precision of its manufacture. Muller currently has another patent pending.

Following the Tourbillon improvement, Franck Muller went on to create five more world premiers, all with the insignia "Franck-Genève," before founding a watchmaking firm with his own name. With his first collection in 1992, he was invited to join the exclusive Salon Internationale de la Haute Horlogerie, whose ranks at the time included only Piaget, Cartier, Baume &

Top: The Franck Muller watchmakers at work in the workshops of Genthod.

Left: Franck Muller Chateau in the village of Genthod, situated on the shores of Lake Geneva.

Above: Franck Muller exclusive movement. Crafted by hand, different components are placed at an angle to obtain optimal precision. The screws in the movement are diamond polished in black and then blued. Each piece calls for special care, so that when each wristwatch leaves the Genthod workshops one can see the great quality of the Genevese workmanship.

Above: ENDURANCE 24 1997 VERSION Manual watch with mechanical movement, self-running 50 hours. Three counter chronograph and tachymeter on bezel. Case in solid stainless steel and screwed down crowns to increase water resistance.

Below: RMQPTR (Minute Repeater, Perpetual Calendar with Retrograde Equation and Tourbillon) Mechanical watch with manual winding, minute repeater striking the hours, the quarters and the minutes on request, indicator of striking mechanism patented by Franck Muller, perpetual calendar, indication of the retrograde monthly equation, indication of the moonphase and 24 hours, Tourbillon patented by Franck Muller, case in solid 18K yellow gold.

Below left: 7000 QPL (Moon Perpetual Calendar) Automatic watch with 950 platinum rotor, hours, minutes, chronograph, perpetual calendar, indication of moonphase and 24 hours, case in solid 18K white gold, water-resistant up to 25 meters.

Below: 2865 NA D CD Manual watch with chronograph, second counter and 30 minute counter, water-resistant 25 meters case in solid yellow gold set with three rows of brilliant cut diamonds and diamond dial.

Mercier and Alfred Dunhill.

By constructing two faces in one timepiece, Franck Muller secured his second patent. The Double Face Chronograph is an exciting wristwatch that displays time-telling features on one side, while the back side features a chronograph with tachometric, telemetric and pulsimetric measures, which allow the wearer to measure speed, distance based on the speed of sound, and

a human's pulse, respectively. The third patent is for his invention improving the indicator of the striking mechanism, which allows the wearer to clearly see whether or not to activate the mechanism.

Through his advancements and complications, Franck Muller secured a niche among the long-standing leaders of the watchmaking industry. The complications provide endless fascination to collectors, not

only because they are devices that ensure a watch keeps the best time, but because they offer specialized information that is not readily apparent to those used to traditional watches. This is particularly true when the watch is a Franck Muller design.

It takes several glances before it becomes clear exactly what the eight dials are registering on the face of the most complicated wristwatch in the world, Muller's

1992 World Premier. On it, the wearer can find the date, day of the week, month, cycle of leap years, moon phases, the internal temperature of the watch and, of course, the time. In addition, the timepiece features a minute-repeater, a grande and petite sonnerie to ring the hour and a perpetual calendar that is programmed up to the year 2100. Who could ask for more? In 1995, Franck Muller did, and he added a Tourbillon.

THE MASTER BANKER Patent pending, this is the first watch in watchmaking history which features three time zones that are operated from a single crown. The dial displays the first time zone (or local time) in the center, the second time zone is shown by an hours and minutes counter at 12 o'clock and the third time zone is shown by an hours and minutes counter at 6 o'clock.

Far left: 7000 MB Automatic watch with 950-platinum rotor, three time zone watch with date indicator at 3 o'clock. Case is made in 18K yellow gold.

Top right: 2852 MB Automatic watch with 950-platinum rotor, three time zone watch with date indicator at 3 o'clock. Case is made in 18K yellow gold.

Sharing a fascination for car racing that is held by many watchmakers, Franck Muller created the Endurance 24 and steered sports watches onto a new track. The wristwatch sports a 24-hour time dial instead of the traditional 12-hour dial. The 1997 version, another world premier, is an automatic split-second chronograph. The time is displayed over 24 hours and features illuminated numbers circling the face, which also includes minute, second and hour counters, as well as a tachometer on the bezel.

Less involved for the wearer, but just as impressive, are the Classic Rounds and Cintrées Curvex collections. Often, these

Left: 7501 CC HV (Havana Manual Chronograph) Designed for a woman's or man's wrist, this is the first medium sized Chronograph since the creation of the brand Franck Muller. A technical imprint enhances the Havana lne with the addition of a chronograph, on which one can read the hours on a dial at 9 o'clock, the minutes at 3 o'clock and the seconds on a dial at 6 o'clock. Hand engraved movement can be viewed through the open case back. Case is in 18K yellow gold and is water-resistant up to 25 meters. .

Above: 6850 CC Automatic Chronograph, chronograph second counter and 30-minute counter enamel dial, water-resistant 25 meters, case in solid 18K yellow gold.

Above: 6850 CCMC (Chronograph Master Calendar) Automatic watch with Chronograph, calendar, royal blue dial, water-resistant 25 meters, case in solid 18K yellow gold.

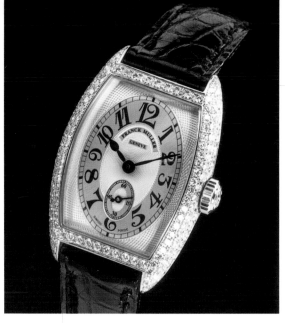

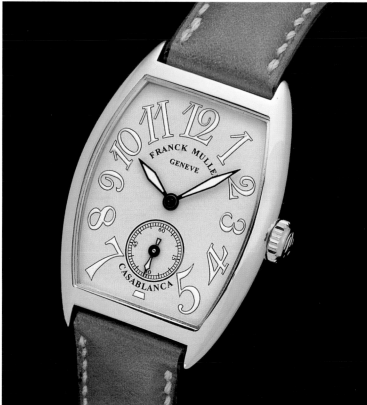

Above: 1751 S6 D CHRONOMETRO (Ladies Diamond Chronometro) Mechanical watch with manual wind up, self-running 40 hours. Hours, minutes and a small seconds dial at 6 o'clock. 18K yellow gold case set with 157 brilliant cut diamonds. (1,455 carats)

Top center: 7501 S6 MM D 2P (Diamond Center Curved) Manual watch with second dial at 6 o'clock, case in solid 18K yellow gold set with three rows of brilliant cut diamonds and 2 diamond circles on dial. water-resistant up to 25 meters.

Top right: 1750 S6 PMD BAGUETTE Mechanical watch with manual winding, case in solid yellow 18K gold, set with baguette diamonds, small second counter, and water-resistant 25 meters.

Right: 5850 CHRONOMETRO (Chronometro) Franck Muller has reinvented this watchmaking classic by creating a new version of the chronometer. Unique in its styling, the Chronometro is an automatic watch with a 950 platinum rotor. With a sweep second hand at center this dial is pictured in an antique rose shade.

Far right: 7502 S6C (Manual Casablanca) Manual watch with a case in 18K yellow gold, salmon dial with luminous figures, seconds dial at 6 o'clock, water-resistant up to 25 meters on a leather strap specially designed for the Casablanca line.

lines are elegant showcases of Muller's ability to solve the problems of those pressed for time. For example, the world premier Master Banker displays on its face, for the first time, three time zones that are set by one crown. Muller says he created the watch for bankers and investors who need to keep up with the stock market closings in New York, London and Tokyo. The timepiece is just as suitable for world travelers.

Muller seemingly knows the wearers of his watches better than they know themselves. His creations are developed in anticipation of their needs and interests. He says he purposefully constructs heavier watches so that his clients are reminded that they are wearing a unique timepiece. His most complicated and exclusive pieces are often self-winding, because he knows true collectors take great pride in caring for the watch.

Personal interests and trends also spark inspiration for his creations. Noticing the surge of interest in cigar smoking, Muller created the Havana collection. It's fired-blue minute and hour hands sweep across an art

deco background with illuminated numerals, all masterfully evoking the spirit of Havana during the 20th Century. The timepiece is neatly housed in a case designed as an oversized replica of a cigar.

Equally impressive is the artistry of his exclusive Cintrée Curvex, its barrel is yet another part advanced by Muller. The tonneau shape is traditionally curved at two points on the watchface. But Muller added additional curves at 3 and 9 to his Cintrée Curvex, further complicating the interior of the watch while at the same time creating a graceful curved timepiece that hugs the wrist. The added curves "give a unique and spherical point of balance" to the watch, says Muller. Enhancing the curvature is a starburst design emanating from the center of the watchface.

As is evidenced by his prolific creations, Franck Muller is not daunted as a relative newcomer to the industry. Already, his production has grown from 300 to 3,500 annually, and it is soon expected to reach 6,000 pieces a year. Muller says he will not expand production further, in order to retain the exclusivity that his watches enjoy. With an increasing presence in the women's market, and a multitude of complications and innovations of his own to draw from — as well as his keen fascination and understanding of watchmaking history — the possibilities are endless.

"I don't have the historical past that long-standing companies have to respect. On the contrary, I can propose an interesting variety of contemporary creations that utilize ancestral know-how," Muller says philosophically. "And don't forget that the company is only five years old, and I am only just beginning."

Girard-Perregaux

WATCHMAKERS for over 200 years, Girard-Perregaux has built an enduring legacy in the most demanding of luxury industries. Renowned for their exacting standards and their adamant refusal to comprise on any aspect of the watchmaking process, the Swiss firm has seduced the most prestigious names in the world, from esteemed individual buyers to Ferrari. The elite Italian car manufacturer collaborated with Girard-Perregaux in 1994 to produce a limited edition "Tribute to Ferrari" series. And in 1995, a full line of "For Ferrari" watches — complete with the famous stallion emblem — was unveiled. The company refers to itself as a "manufactory," emphasizing the fact that Girard-Perregaux is solely responsible for each and every step of a watch's journey, from inception to its final production. Unlike other noted brands, Girard-Perregaux manufactures and assembles their own timepieces. The firm boasts three separate factories in La Chaux-de-Fonds, Switzerland, one for movement making, another for case making and the last for watch assembly.

Previous page: "Tonneau"-shaped Tourbillon with three gold bridges. With it's visible, hand-winding Tourbillon mechanism with three gold bridges, this new masterpiece has a chapter-ring to facilitate reading the time and a small seconds hand integrated into the Tourbillon.

Above: Constant Girard, whose watchmaking firm changed to its present name with his marriage to Marie Perregaux in 1854.

Below: Laureato "Olimpico." Every Olympic year since 1900, Girard Perregaux has produced a chronograph whose lines and features have been inscribed in the annals of the manufactory's history. The Laureato marks the 1996 Olympics.

Bottom right: Laureato Jewelry. The "Laureato for Lady" line has been enriched with precious stones whose baguette- or brilliant-cut underscores the elegant lines of this timeless ladies' watch.

La Chaux-de-Fonds has been a hub for elite watchmaking since the middle of the 18th century, but Girard-Perregaux's own history first began in Geneva in 1791. At this time, J.F Bautte founded a watchmaking studio in his own name in the capital of French-speaking Switzerland. A gifted innovator, he explored the many realms of watchmaking and devised a method for producing extremely thin timepieces. With a burgeoning reputation, the firm passed into the hands of Constant Girard in the mid-1800s. And when Girard married Marie Perregaux in 1854, the legendary moniker of Girard-Perregaux was born.

In 1867, after intensive research on the use of gold in a movement, Girard-Perregaux created a masterpiece: the famous tourbillon with three gold bridges. The tourbillon watch is a technological marvel, whose goal is to correct the inaccuracies a time-piece is subjected to by the negative effects of gravity. The triple-gold bridge model unleashed by Girard-Perregaux was an

Above left: Tourbillon with three gold bridges with minute repeater. Just like the celebrated pocket-watch model, the Tourbillon mechanism is visible through the transparent caseback. The bridges have been reworked to form large arabesques through which one can glimpse the striking mechanism for the hour, quarter and minute repeater, whose delicate chime is activated by moving the slide.

Above: Skeleton Tourbillon with three gold bridges. With this new symbol of watchmaking mastery, the Girard-Perregaux manufactory offers a veritable work of art to both collectors and lovers of unique timepieces. Manufactured entirely in its workshops, the skeleton Tourbillon with three gold bridges joins the prestigious dynasty of these timeless and magical watches.

immediate triumph. At the Paris Universal Exhibitions of 1867 and 1889, the watch was an obvious selection for a gold medal. And, in the ultimate show of respect, organizers of the 1901 exhibition judged the watch too perfect to compete.

In 1981, 20 replicas of the original tourbillon pocket watch with three gold bridges were issued by

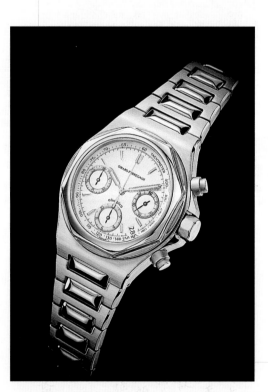

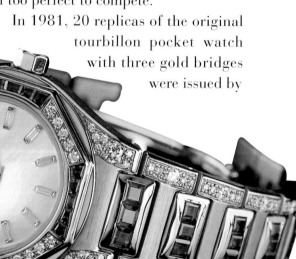

Girard-Perregaux, underscoring the fact that its watchmakers were still masters of the technical know-how needed to execute such complicated works. Each watch required a six- to eight-month production calendar, with much of the labor hours dedicated solely to the arduous process of assembling and adjusting the intricate components.

In celebration of its bicentennial in 1991, Girard-Perregaux adapted its three-gold-bridged tourbillon to a wristwatch format for the first time. Capitalizing on the world's fascination with the exquisite timepiece, Girard-Perregaux introduced a revolutionary wristwatch with a one-bridge tourbillon mechanism fitted into a tonneau-shaped case in 1996. And in 1997, Girard-Perregaux's tireless craftsmen once again surpassed all expectations when they created a tonneau-shaped tourbillon mechanism with three bridges. Produced in a very limited and numbered series, Girard-Perregaux's latest marvel is already the crown of many distinguished private collections.

Girard-Perregaux assures the exquisite quality of each of its creations by producing just 15,000 timepieces a year. 10,000 of these boast the company's own name, while the remaining 5,000 are emblazoned with the distinctive "For Ferrari" seal.

Luigi Macaluso, the present-day owner of Girard-Perregaux, fostered a relationship with Ferrari nearly three decades ago. A professional driver for the Fiat group in the 1970s, Macaluso has been a long-time friend and associate of Ferrari's president,

Top: To mark the manufactory's attachment to its prestigious past, Girard-Perregaux is offering, for the second consecutive year, a limited and numbered series of a replica of a watch from the prolific 1940s. For it's new Vintage, the manufactory has chosen to celebrate the jubilee model it created in 1945.

Above: The first Vintage, created in 1994, is the exact and faithful reproduction of the original, which dates back to 1948.

Top center: Rectangular-shaped Richeville. When the Tonneau-shaped Richeville chronograph was launched in 1993, it was instantly recognized as a timepiece with a strong personality and hailed in Japan as "the year's most beautiful watch." Due to the international success that the Richeville line has enjoyed since, Girard-Perregaux has extended the line with a different shaped watch, manufactured with the same rigor and character: the rectangular-shaped Richeville.

Luca Montezemolo. When Macaluso purchased Girard-Perregaux in 1992, becoming the first Italian CEO of a Swiss watchmaking company, a collaboration with Ferrari seemed natural.

"Because Ferrari is a dream car that is unique to the world, we decided to create something that was for the top collectors," Macaluso said. He signed a co-branding deal with Montezemolo and directed his company in the production of an exclusive "For Ferrari" line, "limited edition timepieces in which what was inside the watch counted just as much as the design," according to Macaluso.

The first generation of Ferrari-inspired watches appeared in 1994, and culminated in 1995 when Girard-Perregaux showcased its one-of-a-kind timepiece adorned with a fabulous Ferrari stallion insignia carved out of ruby. This exquisite collector's watch quickly sold for $150,000.

In 1997 the Ferrari motor company commemorated its 50th year by issuing the fabulous F50, the type of remarkable vehicle that could only exist twice in a century. To share in the celebration, Girard-Perregaux once again joined forces with the Italian automotive legend and created the F50 wrist watch.

Girard-Perregaux chose gold, platinum or titanium for the "chassis," which contains the F50 watch's complex mechanism. Masterfully crafted, the F50 timepiece is a colossal technical feat. It boasts an automatic chronograph with a perpetual calendar, capable of correcting the date, even in leap years, until the dawn of the 22nd century.

Girard-Perregaux issued the Ferrari F50 watch in two very limited series. The first series of 349 was designed for the 349 owners of Ferrari F50 cars. Owners

parameters on quality control, Girard-Perregaux ships 50,000 sophisticated movements a year to other prestigious watch-making brands.

As Luigi Macaluso says of his company, "When you buy a Girard-Perregaux watch, you are buying a piece of a dream, a piece of aesthetics, and finally, of course, a functional item for the telling of time."

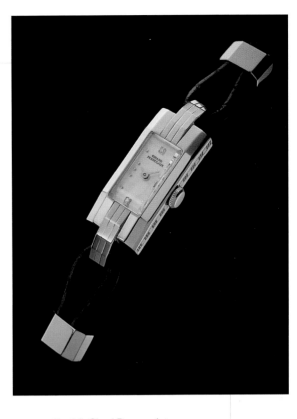

Top left: Girard-Perregaux's tourbillon mechanism with three gold bridges. As part of its bicentenary celebrations in 1991, Girard-Perregaux presented a world first at Basel: a wristwatch version of its tourbillon with three gold bridges.

Above: Vintage Lady, 1997. The remarkable charm of the 30s. Once again, the Girard-Perregaux museum in La Chaux-de-Fonds has been a source of inspiration for the manufactory. It is well known that in the 1930s Girard-Perregaux enjoyed an international reputation for the beauty and elegance of its ladies' watches. This superb timepiece, inspired by a model introduced in 1937, in a very limited series of 250.

Left: Vintage 1997, shaped split seconds chronograph. This model is inspired by a Girard-Perregaux watch made in 1947, exactly 50 years ago. Like all Vintage models, it is available in a limited numbered series.

who acquired the F50 watch were cordially invited by Girard-Perregaux to have their names and the serial number of their automobile engraved on the watch's case. A second series of 250 chronographs was then offered to distinguished collectors.

A complete company, Girard-Perregaux cannot be categorized solely as a manufacturer of grand complications such as the tourbillon mechanism or as a refined collaborator with the likes of Ferrari. They also produce hand-winding and automatic mechanical movements, and an estimated seven percent of their line holds quartz movements. World renowned for their strict

Harry Winston

By DRAWING the craft of watchmaking from the depths of Harry Winston's past, Ronald Winston is guiding three generations of the towering jeweler into the 21st century. Harry Winston is internationally celebrated as the man who bestowed star status on the largest and rarest diamonds, sapphires, emeralds and rubies. His vision, passion and innate knowledge of the gems earned him the title of "King of Diamonds." Yet, the genius of gems was the second generation of a family of jewelers. Harry Winston's father, Jacob Winston, trained as a jeweler and watchmaker in Europe and he was a craftsman foremost, as was his son. In 1890, Jacob Winston opened a small jewelry shop in New York, while at the same time crafting his own clocks and watches. One of the clocks, completely intact with its original parts, sits on the desk of Ronald Winston, son of Harry Winston and president of the jeweler. Today, Ronald Winston muses that his father and grandfather would be proud that the three men together have built a remarkable jeweler and watchmaker of unrivaled stature.

appraisal and purchase of estate jewelry that flooded the market during the roaring 20s. He quickly became the leader of gem dealing, and mine owners sought him as the

Previous page: Ocean watch. The first ever all-platinum diving watch.

Above: Fifth Avenue Ladies' 22mm diamond and precious stone watches in 18K yellow gold.

Far left: Fifth Avenue Ladies' 22mm 18K yellow gold diamond watch with approximately 16.50 carats accompanied by a pear shape diamond ring and diamond earrings.

Below: Fifth Avenue platinum diamond watch – 16.50 carats.

While the family business transcends three generations, its international presence is traced to Harry Winston, who shaped the family business into its status today as America's premier jeweler. After working through his teens at his father's Los Angeles shop, Harry Winston ventured to New York, with a few thousand dollars in savings and a bold enterprising spirit. The 20-year-old quickly built his success through the

authority in determining a gems worth. Harry Winston took great risks, often cutting stones that no one else would, all in the name of exacting the greatest beauty from the stone, while at the same time reducing its flaws. The result was a more valuable, beautiful gem, and for Harry Winston, a burgeoning jewelry firm that grew to international stature spanning from its New York headquarters on Fifth Avenue to salons in Beverly Hills, Paris, Geneva and Tokyo. Since his death in 1978, his son Ronald Winston has been the jeweler's driving force, expanding the family business while contin-

uing to honor his father's tradition.

In 1989, Ronald Winston added watchmaking to the company's repertoire under the Ultimate Timepiece division, based in world center of watchmaking, Geneva, Switzerland. The progression is logical. Not only does Harry Winston trace the craft to its first generation, the development of timepieces ventures into the realm of jewelry, as both are viewed as symbols of achievement. In symmetry with the sparkling gems renowned at Harry Winston, the jeweler and watchmaker has created individual timepieces as magnificent as diamonds or emeralds. The watches also provide a luxurious and fitting complement to Harry Winston's special jewels.

The Ultimate Timepiece features six inimitable collections named in homage to

the finest places in the world: Fifth Avenue, Madison Avenue, Times Square, Indianapolis, Palm Beach and Greenwich.

Appropriately enough, the first woman's timepiece ever created at Harry Winston was a diamond watch, launching the Fifth Avenue collection. Ronald Winston knew from the outset that design would guide the development of the watch and the interior watch workings would simply have to fit the style. The final creation is a glorious timepiece featuring two golden hour hands sweeping across a gleaming face of diamonds, worn on the wrist with a supple, articulated bracelet of streaming diamonds, in four strands or three, supported with yellow gold or platinum. In sparkling variety, the timepieces can be set with rubies, sapphires or emeralds, or, by special order, colored diamonds.

Left: Ladies' Madison watches in 18K white gold with diamonds.

Below: Madison Avenue Ladies' 18K yellow gold diamond watches.

Bottom left: Ladies' Madison watch in 18K white gold with diamond bezel.

Inspiration for high-jewelry watches has since grown to include the dazzling Madison Avenue collection. Slightly sporty and casual, yet distinctly stylish, the Madison line includes the trademark Harry Winston watchface, whose numbers circle the dial in perfect conformity to the round watchface. It is also available with a face dotted with diamonds marking the hour. For the fashion-forward woman on the move, a second version comes with inter-changeable crocodile leather straps. Recent additions

Below: Madison Avenue Ladies' 27mm diamond accent watch in 18K gold with interchangeable straps.

Right: Times Square Gentleman's platinum 34mm watch with crocodile strap.

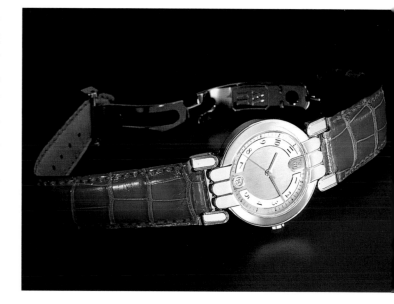

to the Ultimate Timepiece series cater to those at the forefront of society who are seeking good-looking, unique watches that not only feature precision timing, but are also as precious as a favorite item of jewelry.

In this spirit, designers created the Ocean, the first ever all platinum diving watch. The timepiece is now among the top selling watches at Harry Winston. Sporty and rugged, the Ocean is durable and fashionable for any sporting lifestyle. Waterproof to 300 feet, the Ocean's mechanical movement is protected thanks to a screw-down crown. The watch is available with a lorica strap, for the avid diver, or a platinum band. For diving purposes, the Ocean's platinum bezel can be rotated underwater and the time and date indicator at six o'clock are easy to read in luminous tritium.

The thrill of racing is captured in the Indianapolis collection of chronographs, equipped with a Piguet 1185 self-winding mechanical movement that is visible through the transparent back. The wearer is able to record times on a 30-minute and 12-hour subdial and by the center seconds hand through gradations inscribed on the dial rim. At the Basel Fair in 1997, Harry Winston launched one of the most exciting additions to the collection of chronographs, a version that includes a pulsimetric function that can compute cardiac rhythms. Simply by pressing a special button, count-

ing fifteen heartbeats, and pressing the button again, the wearer is provided with an instant readout of his cardiac rhythm. All of the chronographs are available in the link bracelet of 950 platinum or in 18K white or yellow gold with a leather strap.

Always anticipating the needs of today's leaders who must keep on track around the world, designers created the Greenwich collection, which features a dual-time zone feature. An investor in New York never loses sight of the markets in Tokyo. A buyer in Los Angeles keeps the rhythm of the ateliers in Paris. No matter where the mind or heart is, Greenwich tracks both at the whim of the wearer. The time-zone display is brilliantly presented in a traditional 12-hour dial design with a day/night indicator.

On the caseback of each timepiece, Harry Winston's name is delicately engraved.

Left: Pulsimeter Chronograph.

Below: Indianapolis Chronograph 18K yellow gold with crocodile straps.

Bottom left: Greenwich watch.

HARRY WINSTON
The Ultimate Timepiece

Jaeger-LeCoultre

AT THE INCEPTION of modern watchmaking is Jaeger-LeCoultre, the prestigious watchmaker molded and shaped by Antoine LeCoultre, who built his company from the ground up by first developing the very precise tools and mechanisms that precisely craft each movement. It was just a matter of time before LeCoultre & Co. grew into the thriving, highly respected watchmaker that today produces timepieces famous around the world. Perhaps more than any other watchmaker, Jaeger-LeCoultre enjoys the privileged distinction as the reference point for watchmakers. Attesting to Jaeger-LeCoultre's commitment are scores of patents and record-holding developments, from the world's slimmest movement developed in 1903 to the Calibre 101, whose 98 parts are assembled in a movement weighing about a gram, holding the title as world's smallest mechanical watch movement since its development in 1929. And then there is the Reverso. Truly a product of its time, the 1930s timepiece remains contemporary, never losing its distinct delight by displaying or concealing time at the wearer's whim.

Previous page: Reverso Chronographe Rétrograde. 1997. Limited series of 500. Calibre 829.

Top: The millionometer, developed by Antoine LeCoultre in 1844, revolutionized watchmaking by making it possible for the first time to measure one thousandth of a millimeter.

Above: Charles-Antoine LeCoultre founded his own watchmaking firm in 1833.

Right: Calibre 101. 1929. The world's smallest mechanical movement since 1929. Mechanical manually-wound movement. 21,600 v/h, 19 jewels, 98 parts. 3.4 mm high.

Below: Mr. Henry-John Belmont, general manager of the manufacture Jaeger-LeCoultre.

Antoine LeCoultre was born in the Swiss Jura, renowned for the long, harsh winters that fomented a community of craftsman. Often cut off for weeks or months due to the severe weather, the inhabitants of the Vallée de Joux had plenty of time to acquire, and excel at, the highly detailed skills required for watchmaking. The LeCoultre family was no exception and in the town of Le Sentier they began by making razors and music boxes before producing watch components. In 1833, Antoine LeCoultre and his brother started their own business manufacturing watch gearing and Antoine LeCoultre began investing his energy into the development of new production processes. LeCoultre's first invention — the millionometer, which set the meter as the watch industry's standard of measurement — marked the beginning of a revolution in the watchmaking industry. Once dominated by the French and English who needed to provide precise time keeping mechanisms to their merchant and naval fleets, the industry took a turn with the Swiss innovations. In no time, the Swiss manufacturers were constructing more precise timepieces in greater

Left: In the thirties, only the Reverso was able to stand-up to a polo match, a skiing excursion or a daredevil automobile race such as the Mille Miglia in Italy.

numbers, easily overtaking the business from their neighbors.

LeCoultre & Co. rapidly became Le Sentier's top employer, as well as a reliable source for complicated movements, minute repeaters and calendars. Before passing the company down to his three sons, Antoine LeCoultre produced the first keyless winding system, and his gold chronometer featuring the keyless winding stole the top prize, the gold medal, at the Great Exhibition in London in 1851.

Each generation of the LeCoultre family contributed toward expanding production and raising the company's level of prestige. Antoine LeCoultre's three sons, Elie, Paul and Benjamin focused on modernizing the facilities, such as adding electricity and purchasing a steam engine. This significantly boosted production levels so that by 1890, the company was producing a range of 125 different movements. Elie LeCoultre was first to advocate the

manufacturing of complete timepieces. And it was Elie's son, Jacques-David LeCoultre, who forged partnerships that would change the face — and the name — of the family business. The 22-year-old immersed himself in the business as soon as he finished watchmaking school. At his urging, the craftsmen began crafting wondrous movements, including the world's smallest movement, perfect for the fashionable timepieces of minute or unusual shapes that began emerging during the Art Deco period. Jacques-David LeCoultre possessed a great acumen for sales and marketing and he began developing many friendships worldwide that increased prominence for LeCoultre & Co. His friendships with the entrepreneurial marketing wizard César de Trey and French watchmaker

Edmond Jaeger produced marvels ranging from the renowned Reverso wristwatch to the Atmos clock, powered by changes in air temperature. Both are still in production today. César de Trey is also credited with convincing LeCoultre to produce timepieces under the watchmakers own name, selling its movements to other fine watchmakers. The French watchmaker, Edmond Jaeger, another associate of Jacques-David LeCoultre, helped his friend tap the French luxury market, selling his movements to names like Cartier.

Early on, Jaeger and LeCoultre joined forces to market the Duoplan, popular wristwatches with an extraordinary guarantee by Lloyds of London, who insured the watches against theft, loss, destruction or irreparable damage. By 1937, Jaeger & LeCoultre officially merged, although the two names had been appearing together on watch faces for sometime.

Three names, LeCoultre, Jaeger, and de Trey, are behind the most magnificent story in watchmaking history. It is the story of the Reverso, one of the

Top left: Two faces, one movement: Jaeger-LeCoultre creates the Reverso Duetto. A classic front: silvered guilloché dial, enhanced with "floral" numerals. A sparkling back: silvered guilloché and mother-of-pearl dial, case set with 32 full-cut diamonds. Mechanical manually-wound movement and double hand-fitting. Calibre 844. Stainless steel. Crocodile strap with folding buckle. 266.842.443B
Stainless steel and 18K gold. Crocodile strap with folding buckle. 266.542.443B

Above: Reverso Duetto. 18K gold set with 168 diamonds. Crocodile strap with gold folding buckle. 266.142.001B Calibre 844.

Left: Reverso Joaillerie. 18K white gold case and bracelet set with 346 diamonds and 24 emeralds. 267.997.862 Calibre 846.

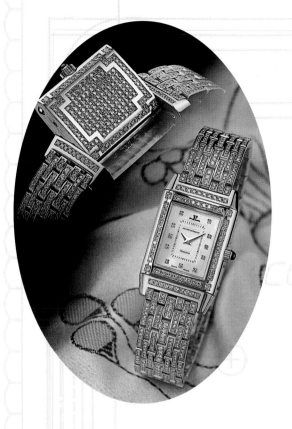

Above: Reverso Joaillerie.
18K yellow gold set with 998
diamonds.
267.110.001
Calibre 846.

Top right: The Reverso Bague
(ring) is accompanied by a
matching necklace and earring
set, echoing the Art Deco
design of the legendary
swivel watch.

Bottom right: Reverso Florale.
Stainless steel set with
diamonds. Crocodile strap
with folding buckle.
265.842.082B
Calibre 608.

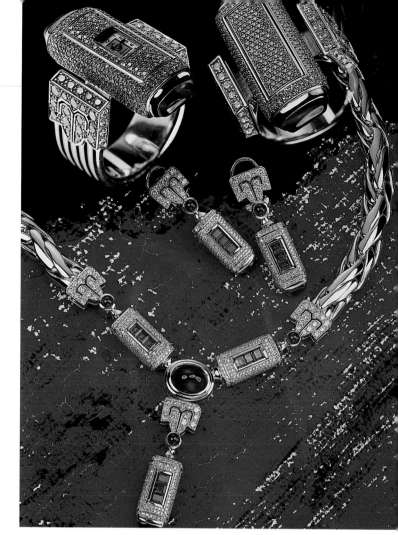

few items from the Art Deco era that lives on, despite that its original practicality is outmoded. The Reverso idea was born on a Polo field. During a visit to India, César de Trey went to a Polo match, after which he listened to the players bemoan the loss of their watch glass, which easily cracked during the game. One player asked whether César de Trey could produce a watchface that could be turned over to protect the fragile glass. César de Trey immediately grasped the brilliance of the idea, and he made LeCoultre his first stop back in Europe. Jacques-David LeCoultre embraced the idea, but he realized his company did not yet have the expertise to create the watchface. Shortly after the two men met, Jacques-David LeCoultre headed to Paris, to discuss the plan with Edmond Jaeger, whose engineers also took an immediate liking to the plan.

The engineering of the watch, and its pivoting mechanism in particular, is quite demanding and highly sophisticated. But the first Reversos appeared in 1931, just one year after the meeting on the polo field, just in time for Christmas. The fashionable timepiece was an instant hit, high society was still immersed in the spirit of the roaring 20s and the Reverso drew attention to itself at cocktail parties. Whenever someone asked for the time, the protective backing would be flipped to tell the hour, then flipped again, banishing time from sight. The protective caseback immediately became a format for expression.

paintings, including a marvelous Art Nouveau representation of the four seasons.

Even after crystal replaced the fragile glass, the playfulness of the Reverso endured for years. In the 1970s, the timepiece made a comeback after gentle prodding by the manufacturer's Italian representative, Giorgio Corvo. He'd noticed that other Art Deco items were gaining popularity and he ordered all the remaining Reversos. The problem was, Jaeger-LeCoultre was no longer producing the movements. Worse yet, the equipment used to produce the Reverso had been dismantled and its design blueprints, destroyed. Engineers had to start from scratch to begin producing the watch, a development that took three years.

Almost ten years later, designers would revamp the timepiece to make technological improvements. Yet the construction is virtually the same as the original, and Jaeger-LeCoultre remained dedicated to its firm commitment of fitting the case with a movement that fits its rectangular shape.

As early as 1937, engineers had experimented with a retrograde-calendar, month, day and moon phase version of

Jaeger-LeCoultre's artists began engraving the owner's initials on the metal plate. And when César de Trey returned to India in homage to the Reverso's birthplace, a new idea sprang forth. The maharajah of Karputala wanted a painting of himself and his wife to appear on the back. Artists and designers teamed up and decided to recreate the painting in enamel on the caseback. The stunning results inspired several enamel

the Reverso, but it never left the prototype stage. In 1991, the Reverso became officially complicated in celebration of its 60th birthday, and all 500 versions of the Reverso 60éme were sold within months. Now, instead of monograms on the caseback, connoisseurs and collectors can admire complications through the sapphire crystal on the caseback. Such is the case with the Reverso Tourbillon, a marvel to view, the cage's 70 parts weigh less than half a gram.

Like the Reverso, the Master Control 1000 Hours watches are masterpieces rich in history. The names like Memovox,

Above: Reverso Enamel, "Quatre Saisons." Based on Alphonse Mucha's "Four Seasons," each season is portrayed in an enamel miniature on the back of the legendary Reverso watch by Jaeger-LeCoultre's master-enamaller. 18K gold, crafted in a limited series of 25.

Top right: Master Perpetual and Master Geographic in platinum with deep blue dial, in a limited series of 250.

Bottom center: Reverso Duo. 18K white gold. Crocodile strap with white gold folding buckle. 270.240.544. Calibre 854.

Futurematic or Geomatic that emerged in the 50s are at the origin of Master Control, a series of watches designed to attain the pinnacle of reliability. Jaeger-LeCoultre subjects the timepieces to the toughest and longest testing program —1000 hours — to ensure that it will last two generations. Each year, a new edition is proudly presented. Among the most recent are the platinum editions of the Master Geographic and Master Perpetual. Engineers have worked the hands of time to create the Master Geographic, which shows the local time and the hour in another time zone. The timepiece also includes a related, unique feature: a time zone disc. The dial, located above the 6, displays time in the secondary time zone.

The Master Perpetual is testimony to the rigorous testing subjected to the 1000 hours series of watches. Its self-adjusting date knows the months with 30 and 31 days, and

Left: Calibre 929/3. 1996. Mechanical automatic movement with date, power-reserve indicator and a 24-hour second time zone. 28,800 v/h. 38 jewels, 293 parts, 4.85 mm high.

Bottom left: (top) Calibre 889/440/2. 1996. Mechanical automatic movement with perpetual calendar. 28,800 v/h, 50 jewels, 277 parts. 4.55 mm high. (bottom) Calibre 918. 1994. Mechanical automatic movement with date and mechanical alarm, incorporating a gong. 28,800 v/h. 22 jewels, 260 parts, 7.45 mm high.

Above: Master Réserve de Marche. Stainless steel. Ostrich strap with folding buckle. 140.840.932B Calibre 928. (right) Master Réveil. Stainless steel. Ostrich strap with folding buckle. 141.840.972B Calibre 918.

Left: Robert Kohler transported the Atmos beyond earth-bound time in the Atmos Atlantis. Suspended in its crystal-clear capsule, the Atmos Atlantis seems to float weightlessly in space. Based on a 1928 invention, its energy is supplied by variations in temperature. A difference of one degree will keep the movement going for 48 hours.

accounts for the leap years, beyond the new millennium.

Such expertise at linking the past to the future is what sets Jaeger-LeCoultre apart from most other watchmakers. From the Reverso's independent manner of telling the time to the technological advancements of the Atmos clock, Jaeger-LeCoultre inspires within its talented craftsmen and engineers a unique dedication.

The result is magical for collectors and connoisseurs, who consider ownership of the timepieces with the esteemed name Jaeger-LeCoultre as great fortune.

Omega

MARKING mankind's greatest moments and performances, from man's first step on the moon to the Olympic competitions, Omega watches have been consistently sought by those who demand the most precise timekeeping mechanisms known to mankind. Since its founding in 1848 by Louis Brandt, Omega has reigned as the supreme symbol of Swiss watchmaking, attaining the highest of accolades. In 1900, at the Paris World Fair, experts awarded Omega's entire line the jury's Grand Prix for excellence. For the 1932 Los Angeles Olympics, Omega was named official timekeeper and has been responsible for timekeeping for 23 Olympic games. In 1970, NASA's astronauts awarded their highest distinction, the Snoopy Award, to Omega's Speedmaster, whose precision guided the troubled Apollo 13 mission home. Celebrating in 1998 its 150th Anniversary, the watchmaker maintains the names Constellation, Seamaster, Speedmaster and De Ville as renowned symbols of the name Omega, the last letter of the Greek alphabet and the eternal symbol of consumate excellence and perfection.

Previous page: The Omega Central Tourbillon, the world's first self-winding central tourbillon wristwatch. Case and bracelet in 18K white gold set with 324 diamonds (total 37 carats).

Center right: Record Chronometer. The famous "Omega" 19-line calibre, created in 1894, became the firm's reference for all succeeding movements and the namesake of the company.

Bottom, from left: Poster dating from the 1932 Olympics in Los Angeles. Photofinish of women's 100-meter event at the 1988 Seoul Olympic games.

Left: "Greek Temple" watch, in chased solid gold. Among Omega's complete collection that was awarded the international jury prize at the Paris World Fair in 1900.

Right: Design and Perfection. Salvador Dali statuette table clock, "The Premonition of the Drawers." The artist chose Omega for his symbol of time.

Just as the Swiss Confederation established itself, Louis Brandt began his relentless pursuit of precision timekeeping. In 1848, he opened his workshop in La Chaux-de-Fonds, Switzerland and began assembling high-precision pocket watches. In 1880 his sons, Louis Paul and César, moved the workshops of "Louis Brandt & Fils" to the more modern city of Bienne and began revolutionizing the world of watchmaking. With manpower, electricity and communication lines at their fingertips, the two abandoned the assembly workshop system, established a manufacturing plant and began producing interchangeable parts. The company became the first to produce high precision watches at competitive prices.

The change to the name Omega came in 1894, with the development of the famous "Omega" 19-line caliber. A reference for all succeeding calibers, it became the benchmark for Omega, a brand that would begin ticking off innumerable achievements. In tribute to its Greek name, its watchmakers developed the "Greek Temple" watch to present at the Paris World Fair in 1900, and the entire collection of Omega watches won the prize for excellence at the competition.

Each succeeding generation perfected what those had mastered before. As timekeeping moved to the wrist, Omega's 30-mm

caliber came to symbolize what the 19-line caliber had been to pocket watches: precision, with the top awards to prove it. In 1946, Omega won the highest score ever attained by a wrist chronometer, as well as the brand's 100,000th chronometer ratings certificate.

Already, professionals were seeking out Omega to record the most important

events. In Los Angeles in 1932, Omega was named official timekeeper of the Olympic Games, a position it has held for 60 years. Omega is a leader in innovations for those nail-biting competitive moments, and has also adapted to the changes in technology. Omega developed the first Photo finish camera to record within 1/1000th of a second— as well as the world's first electronic timing — and the brand was first to present elapsed race timing on television screens. Such innovations are the reason Omega continues to

record the world's most important competitions, from the Olympics and America's Cup to the CART World Series (Championship Auto Racing Teams). For the latter, Omega's engineers developed a state-of-the-art system that times and scores race cars, and also presents the race officials, race teams, press and television with instantaneous information during the race. The system tracks the cars as they travel at speeds over

Left: Constellation Chronometer watch in 18K gold. With its forceful lines, its famous 12-sided dial, its Dauphine hands and small appliqué star, the Constellation created in 1952 gains worldwide recognition as one of Omega's finest timepieces.

Far left: Omega Central Tourbillon, a world premiere. Case in 18K yellow, pink or white gold. Self-winding tourbillon movement. Metallized hour and minute hands painted on two revolving sapphire crystals. Silver-plated 18K gold dial with guilloché decor. Water-resistant to 30 meters. Alligator strap.

Above: Still with the look of the original "Moon Watch," the new Speedmaster CART Racing watch is markedly sportive and contemporary in design. A model endorsed by OMEGA ambassador Michael Andretti, one of CART racing's greatest champions, with 35 victories. Self-winding mechanical movement 1143.

Left, bottom: The 24" Split-Seconds Chronograph developed to measure the sports performances of the 1932 Olympic games in Los Angeles. Limited series of 50 pieces in platinum. Antique hand-winding movement, anti-reflective scratch-resistant sapphire crystal. Platinum crown, silvered dial with different levels, guilloché decor and applied hour markers. Water-resistant to 30 meters.

Below: The commemorative Speedmaster in platinum skeletonized version. Limited series launched in 1994, individually numbered and engraved: "Omega Speedmaster Professional Limited Edition 1/50." Satin-finished case middle engraved: "Apollo XI 1969-1994." Platinum bracelet or black Louisiana crocodile leather strap.

Left: Man lands on the moon in 1969 wearing the Omega Speedmaster.

Left below: Historical record of one of the Speedmasters worn during the Apollo VII flight around the moon (December 21-27, 1968).

Below: Speedmaster Professional. The "Moon Watch" features a new steel bracelet which has the original design of the sixties version. Mechanical hand-winding chronograph, movement 1861.

230 miles per hour, and the system database is constantly updated with information and statistics about the race and racers. These advancements prove that Omega is not content to merely perfect timekeeping, Omega also perfects the way mankind witnesses the milestones of time.

"One small step for man. One giant leap forward for mankind." When Neil Armstrong uttered those words, an Omega Speedmaster circled his wrist and ensured the precision of man's first trip to the moon on July 21, 1969. No small feat for man or machine, the Speedmaster Professional had undergone the most rigorous testing thinkable in a blind test against several chronographs by other leading watchmakers: each watch was subjected to 11 different tests, including extremes in temperature (160°F for 48 hours, followed by 30 minutes at 200°F, and 0°F over four hours). The watches were also subjected to six shocks of 40 g's, 11 milliseconds in duration, in six different directions, as well as high pressure, humidity and vibration. The Speedmaster Professional continued to accompany all manned space flights, and in April of 1970 guided the Apollo 13 astronauts back to earth after their systems had shut down. In recognition of the timepiece's precision, NASA's astronauts awarded the Speedmaster the highest honor for person's outside of the U.S. space agency, the "Snoopy" Award. Since 1975, the timepiece has also been part of the standard equipment for Russian Cosmonauts, and this year Omega plans to

Far left: Michael and Ralf Schumacher, two ambassadors of Omega and the leading Formula One drivers today, at the presentation of the newest Omega Speedmaster.

Left: A scale model of two Formula One racing tires, made of genuine material, house the Speedmaster Racing watch, in yellow or red.

Below: The new Omega Speedmaster automatic day-date AM/PM in 18K pink gold is the most recent addition to the collection Speedmaster, successors to the legendary Moon Watch. Case and crown in 18K pink gold. Exclusive self-winding mechanical movement OMEGA 1151. Date, day, month and AM/PM display.

release the X-33, a multi-function watch for use in the shuttle cabin. The timepiece continues to undergo unheard of testing. Last year, cosmonauts aboard the Russian space station MIR tested 35 Speedmaster chronographs in zero-gravity with perfect results.

From space exploration to the racetrack, the Speedmaster Professional is essential to measuring the fractions of seconds that make a crucial difference. The "Moon Watch," as the Speedmaster is known as the "one and only watch to have gone to the moon," assumes a sportier image with the newer models developed with racing in mind. Both Michael Schumacher — the world's fastest Formula One racer — and his brother Ralf wear the Omega watch during competition. As company ambassadors, they presented the newest Speedmaster Professional chronograph series: the Speedmaster automatic date, with a date window at the three; the Speedmaster automatic day-date, with a large date hand stemming from the center, day and month window under the twelve and an integrated 24-hour indicator by the nine in the seconds ring; and the Speedmaster automatic day-date "AM-PM," with its bicolored blue and

black 24-hour scale indication circle, which allows one to differentiate between the morning, afternoon and night hours at a glance. The new models are equipped with an exclusive Omega self-winding mechanical movement.

Calling the Automatic Day-Date AM/PM "the Formula One" of timepieces,

Michael Schumacher says his thrill for sheer precision, speed and passion for racing make it a pleasure and a necessity to wear the new chronograph. In tribute to Michael Schumacher's racing success, Omega has developed a special series of the new automatic models, in bright colors, boxed in a case comprised of two replica's of Formula One wheels. If the Speedmaster is the king of the road, the Omega Seamaster is the ultimate timepiece of the seas. Omega's diving watch, the Seamaster has been setting records since 1932, when Omega's first diving watch the "Marine" went 14 meters underwater, "where the pressure is twice as great as normal." Year after year, the records mounted. Again in 1970, a new world endurance record was set when three divers from Mission Janus spent eight days at 250 meters depth in the Corsican Gulf of Ajaccio exploring the ocean floor. Above water, Omega is the official timekeeper of all important sailing events, including the America's Cup, and is worn by the world's best sailors, such as Sir Peter Blake and his crew of Team New Zealand.

The Seamaster Professional Chrono Diver, is the world's first mechanical diver chronograph-chronometer capable of func-

tioning to a depth of 300 meters, a feat recognized with an official chronometer certificate from the Swiss Chronometer Testing Institute. In 1996 Omega launched its new Constellation, the fashion line of Omega worn by movie stars, trendsetters and world leaders since 1952. Today the Constellation has a wide range of ladies models and an

Above: The Speedmaster Automatic day-date AM/PM, worn by top CART driver and Omega ambassador Michael Andretti.

Top right: DeVille Tonneau. Self-winding Omega movement 1120, with circular-grained, rhodium-plated finish with Geneva wave decoration. Chronometer certificate.

Bottom right: The New Omega Dynamic. Designed to appeal to a young audience of adventure lovers. Its black dial (specially shaped yellow Arabic numerals, white minute track with yellow luminous markers) is inspired by a famous pilot watch used from 1930-1960. Self-winding mechanical movement Omega 1138 with rhodium-plated finish. Chronograph with 60-second and 30-minute totalizers. Anti-reflective, scratch-resistant sapphire crystal.

Langer, Michael and Ralf Schumacher, Michael Andretti, 1997 CART champion Alex Zanardi, as well as personalities in the fashion and movie world, Cindy Crawford, Pierce Brosnan and "James Bond 007."

Each Omega ambassador is chosen because they share the Omega spirit of individual achievement, professional striving and unique personality.

Omega celebrates its 150th anniversary by looking into its glorious past of innovation and entrepreneurship in watchmaking to build a future of even greater achievements.

exclusive collection of high precision models for men. The new Constellation has found in Cindy Crawford the quintessential "Renaissance woman," its ideal spokesperson representing beauty, reliability, fashion and individuality.

Omega has long attracted leaders in the world of sports, science, fashion and politics. But Omega has taken this relationship one step further, and as it celebrates its 150th anniversary in 1998, it does so with a host of leading athletes — Sir Peter Blake, Ernie Els, Martina Hingis, Bernhard

Top left: Cindy Crawford with Nicolas G. Hayek, Chairman of the Board SMH, Cap d'Antibes, France,1997; Bernhard Langer tees off the top of the Washington Square Park arch in New York City for Omega's charity golf event.

Far left, top and below: The top of the Constellation jewelry range, the ladies' model features a diamond-coated dial, bracelet, case, bezel and claws, each set in 18K gold. Below, the Constellation is also available in 18K gold, the bezel is set with diamonds, housing an exclusively Omega quartz movement.

Far left, center: Seamaster Professional Diver Watch, worn by James Bond: Made in stainless steel, the watch is equipped with a self-winding mechanical movement with chronometer certificate. Its unidirectional turning bezel is in aluminum. Helium escape valve. Blue dial, skeleton hands with tritium, anti-reflective, scratch-resistant sapphire crystal. Water-resistant to 300 meters.

Bottom right: The Seamaster 200m with the new Omega Ω-matic movement 1400 unites the precision of quartz with a self-winding recharging system. No battery required and a potential energy reserve of six days. Screw-in crown and caseback, water-resistant to 200 meters, unidirectional turning bezel.

Patek Philippe

IT COULD BE SAID that time is on the side of Patek Philippe, a continuous creator of timepieces since 1839. As a long-time setter of standards in the world of watchmaking, Patek Philippe produces timepieces that claim the top spots in value at auction. In 1989, Patek Philippe auctioned its renowned Calibre 89, the world's most complicated timepiece, for an earthshaking, record-setting $3.2 million. And its 1939 Calatrava astronomical watch with minute-repeater and perpetual calendar, sold for more than $1.7 million in 1996 — 53 years after it was made — making it the most expensive wristwatch ever auctioned. From the outset, Patek Philippe discerned that mankind holds dearest those treasures built by hand. Even in this era of high technology, Patek Philippe's craftsman bring to life, by hand, renowned movements and timepieces. The company's illustrious history began with Antoine Norbert de Patek, who emigrated from Poland and made Geneva his home in exile in the 1830s.

Previous page: The Patek Philippe Calibre 89 – the most complicated portable timepiece ever made. The first Calibre 89 in yellow gold was started in 1980 and completed for the company's 150th anniversary after four years of research, development, and mathematical calculations and five years of construction. Since then, three more pieces have been finished. One each in rose gold, white gold and platinum.

Below: Antoine Norbert de Patek, a Polish watch enthusiast, decided to make Geneva his home in exile, where he started a small watch-making workshop. Adrien Philippe, inventor of the revolutionary crown-winding and setting system that made keys obsolete.

Seizing the vibrancy of the watchmaking industry, he began purchasing precision movements, and, with a certain artistry pulsing through his spirit, he had the casings designed under his direction. He forged a highly successful, albeit brief, partnership with compatriot Franciszek Czapek under the name Patek, Czapek & Co., during which time Patek met Adrien Philippe, a French watchmaker who had successfully mastered the development of a timepiece that could be wound and set without a key. Patek, Czapek & Co. was producing a similar timepiece, but without the same level of technical success. So impressed was Patek with the revolutionary development that he immediately appointed him as technical director.

Shortly afterward, Patek and Czapek ended their business partnership. Philippe

Top center: Queen Victoria (1819-1901) with her Patek Philippe, which is one of the first keyless watches incorporating Adrien Philippe's integrated winding and setting. The blue enamel matched the color of the Queen's eyes. Below center: Richard Wagner (1813-1883) chose this elegant quarter-repeating watch in 1862, while living near Lucerne. Right: Albert Einstein (1879-1955) ordered this ultra-slim pocket-watch with an engraved case and easily readable numerals in 1915. Bottom right: Marie Curie (1867-1934): Flowers and a dream landscape painted in enamels adorn this beautiful watch made by Patek Philippe in 1895.

naturally assumed the role as partner, and in 1845 the watchmaker attained the first of more than 60 patents to come with the production of Philippe's keyless watch. In January of 1851, the two forged the abiding name Patek Philippe, and months later the future of the company was sealed at the Great Exhibition in London, where Queen Victoria chose for herself one of the first keyless winding timepieces. A blue enameled piece with a floral motif, exquisitely decorated with diamonds, it is said to have matched the young Queen's eyes. Such

Left: The best known Calatrava, ref. 3919 for men and ref. 4809 for ladies, with the original hobnail bezel, has become the identity of Patek Philippe watchmaking. Here the ref. 4820/1 for ladies is set with diamonds (approx. 0.90 ct).

endorsement was repeated by nobility and dignitaries worldwide, and Patek Philippe's early customers reads as a 'Who's Who' of the time: Albert Einstein, Marie Curie, Leo Tolstoy and Richard Wagner.

From the invention of the first Swiss wristwatch in 1867 to innumerable innovations and new movements of today, Patek Philippe continues to pursue its founding philosophy and commitment to design, produce and assemble the world's finest watches.

In 1932 the Stern family, long-time dial manufacturers for Patek Philippe, acquired the watchmaker with a commitment to preserving

the rock-solid tradition and stability that enabled the company to survive the toughest challenges. Within two years, they had significantly expanded Patek Philippe's markets and had established a New York office to distribute the watch in America. Now Philippe Stern is at the helm of the company, running a network that has since expanded to its present size of 500 authorized retailers in 67 countries worldwide.

Today, Patek Philippe's watches continue to test the limits of time, the parts of each timepiece are hand finished, reducing friction and ensuring that the watch will last generations. What's more, Patek Philippe can make parts for its older timepieces, an assurance to every watch collector that their investment will continue to function at an optimum level. As further testimony to its tradition of endurance, the watchmaker's classic Calatrava line has been the company's best seller for nearly a century. It is one of the six families of wristwatches produced at Patek Philippe, including the Nautilus, Neptune, Ellipse, Gondolo, and the Flamme watches for women — not to mention, of course, Patek Philippe's

Above: From the invention of the first Swiss wristwatch in 1867 to innumerable innovations and new movements of today, Patek Philippe continues to pursue its founding philosophy and commitment to design, produce and assemble the world's finest watches. In 1932 the Stern family, long-time dial manufacturers for Patek Philippe, acquired the watchmaker with a commitment to preserving the rock-solid tradition and stability that enabled the company to survive the toughest challenges. Within two years, they had significantly expanded Patek Philippe's markets and had established a New York office to distribute the watch in America. Now Philippe Stern is at the helm of the company, running a network that has long since expanded to its present size of 500 authorized retailers in 67 countries worldwide.

Left: The first known Swiss wristwatch. Unique, 18K gold bangle watch with 6 line rectangular movement, cylinder escapement. Key winding. Note the two carat old-cut diamond set into the spring-cover over an enamel dial.

Above, from left: As a tribute to Art Deco, Patek Philippe introduced the Gondolo collection as an authentic design expression for the 1990's. Pictured here are ref. 5024 for men with our mechanical movement, and diamond-set (approx. 0.57) ref. 4825/20 for ladies' with a quartz movement. Both are water resistant to 25 meters.

Top center and below: The Golden Ellipse, with its smooth elliptical bezel, is one of the most distinctive and highly sought-after Patek Philippe designs. It remains as fresh and stunning as the day it was introduced in 1968. Pictured above right are men's classical ref. 3978 and 3848/22 with mechanical movements. The stunning ladies' watch, ref. 4832, in 18K yellow gold is entirely paved with diamonds (approx. 1.7 cts). The mobile attachments fit the wrist comfortably and beautifully. All are water resistant to 25 meters.

celebrated complicated watches. Since its debut in 1932, the Calatrava watches have enjoyed celebratory status as a favorite among the men's and women's wristwatches. The round-cased classic wristwatch is named after the ornate, medieval cross, whose image appears discretely on the winding crown.

Each of the families of watches enjoy a certain history that is possible only through such an enduring company as Patek Philippe. Geometric shapes of the Art Deco period set the stage for the Gondolo timepieces, styled in the rectangular or tonneau shapes popular during the 30s and 40s. Originally designed for the Gondolo & Labourian firm in Rio de Janeiro, Brazil, the watches of this era are much sought after at auction. Also inspired by geometric harmony is the sleek style of the "Ellipse" watch, its inspiration from the ancient principal known as the golden section. Its elliptical bezel creates a graceful timepiece for evening that is also classical for daytime.Its design is as original today as it was in 1968 when it was first introduced.

A masterpiece of design and watchmaking technique, the Nautilus is an extraordinary example of thoughtful creativity

One can not imagine the excitement at Patek Philippe when chainsmiths discovered a box of beautiful ladies' bracelets in the 1960s, each bracelet depicting an unusual flame pattern. In the 1980s, they began studying one of the bracelet designs to determine how the pattern was developed. After several years of development, the sinuous pattern from a single gold wire, weaved into a gold chain, was finally recreated, and Patek Philippe introduced the "Flamme" line of watches. The process to produce them is so exclusive, each theme is interpreted by the chainsmith who creates it, meaning no two "Flamme" timepieces are the same.

Most recently, Patek Philippe has been generating excitement within the watch world with its production of complicated timepieces. As a result, whenever the word complication comes up, so, too, does the name Patek Philippe, immediately followed by mention of the Calibre 89. Widely regarded as one of the most complicated watches in the world with its 1,728 parts and 33 complications, the timepiece is also credited with reigniting what was a flagging interest in complications. Unveiled in celebration of the watchmaker's 150th birthday, the Calibre 89 sold at auction for an unprecedented $3.2 million, or roughly $974 for each day of the nine years it took to research, develop, and assemble the masterpiece.

at every level. At first glance, it is immediately apparent that the porthole-shaped watchface is designed for those who love the ocean. In 1976, the Nautilus became Patek Philippe's first sports watch capable of withstanding water pressure to 120 meters, the ladies' watch withstands pressure to 60 meters. Its seal and water-resistance are ensured by four lateral screws. While it is one of Patek Philippe's most practical sports watches, its elegance is suitable for any event, day or night. Twenty years later, Patek Philippe presented its second family of elegant sport watches with the Neptune line. It's round watchface is surrounded by starburst rays on its bezel, providing a streamlined elegance for the active person.

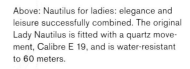

Above: Nautilus for ladies: elegance and leisure successfully combined. The original Lady Nautilus is fitted with a quartz movement, Calibre E 19, and is water-resistant to 60 meters.

Top left: The original Nautilus in 18K gold and the Nautilus on a leather strap are both fitted with the self-winding movement, Calibre 330 SC, with sweep-seconds and date. Water-resistant to 120 meters.

Far left: The Neptune Collection is a new leisure watch, ideal for sportswear yet supremely elegant. This ladies' Neptune ref. 4881/120 in 18K yellow gold has a bezel with 36 diamonds (approx. 1.04 cts) and diamonds on its bracelet. Quartz movement. Water-resistant to 60 meters.

Below center: The extraordinarily supple, sinuous flame-patterned bracelet that gives this collection its name was originally created in the early years of this century. No two Flamme bracelets are exactly the same. Each is created entirely by hand from 18K gold wire. The spectacular diamond-set (approx. 1.10 cts) ref. 4815/3 has delicate hands of twisted gold and diamond hour-markers. Water-resistant to 25 meters.

Any fan of numbers and mechanics will appreciate the mind-boggling features of the Calibre 89: two main dials and 24 hands show the hours, minutes and seconds in sidereal time, solar time and a conversion to conventional time; the time for sunrise and sunset; time in a different time zone; a celestial chart displays the evolution of the sky (changeable depending upon geographical location of the wearer); an astronomical calendar; a split-action chronograph, and much, much more, including, of course, a tourbillon. Patek Philippe produced a total of four timepieces, one each in yellow gold, rose gold, white gold and platinum.

On the heels of such tremendous success, other watchmakers began increasing their production of complications, so Patek Philippe switched gears and began developing useful complications for the lower price watch range. One of the resulting creations is the first self-winding annual calendar wristwatch, the Ref. 5035 is patented and the recipient of the 1996-97 "Watch of the Year" award. Its concept contrasts with the popular date watches, which must be changed five times a year, during the months that have fewer than 31 days, while the Ref. 5035 wristwatch must be changed only once, at the end of February. For each complication that is added to a timepiece, the level of difficulty increases in production. For this reason, the reference 5016 is billed as a masterpiece. A tourbillon wristwatch with minute repeater, perpetual calendar with fly-back date hand and phase of the moon, it is the first to combine all of the complications in a wristwatch. The ingenious development of a spiral-coiled spring allows the calendars fly-back date hand to swing back to the beginning of the month every time, with no margin of error.

Years of research produced the first minute repeater to sound with the authentic chime sound of pocket watches, a remarkable feat given the difference in size.

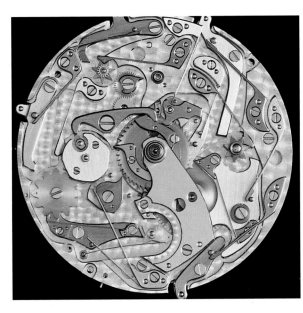

Above: Calibre 315 S QA self-winding movement with annual calendar mechanism. 316 parts. On March 1, 1996, Patek Philippe was granted a Swiss patent for a unique horological mechanism, the self-winding annual calendar, making ref. 5035 the first watch of its kind.

Left: The calibre RTO 27 PS QR is a masterpiece made of 506 components.

Bottom left: The first time in the 500-year history of watchmaking that one wristwatch has been made to combine all of the splendid complications that constitute the enthusiast's dream: a tourbillon, a minute repeater, a perpetual calendar, with fly-back date hand, and the phases of the moon. Ref 5016 is the most complicated wristwatch in Patek Philippe's current production.

Bottom center: The Annual Calendar, ref 5035, was chosen as Watch of the Year, 1996/1997 in Switzerland, and features the calibre 315 S QA, shown above. In yellow gold, rose gold or platinum. 316 parts.

Avid sports fans eagerly awaited the split seconds chronograph wristwatch, with perpetual calendar and moon phase. The split seconds chronograph allows the wearer to record the speeds of two different events at the same time. What's more, the chronograph incorporates a fly-back hand, so that each event is recorded without disturbing the intermediate times. Meanwhile, the perpetual calendar is accurate to February 28, 2100, if the wristwatch is kept wound. The precision of the moon phase keeps the dial accurate for 122 years before the wearer would incur an error of a single day.

Such innovations have been pleasing watch connoisseurs for decades, and they are the result of

exacting diligence on the part of Patek Philippe. Craftsmen must have minimum of four to six years apprenticeship before entering the doors of the watchmaker's workshops. The firm allows plenty of time for the development of every timepiece, and it is followed up by rigorous testing. Then each watch is individually numbered and recorded into the companies records, including everything from who made the timepiece to who purchased it. Finally, for collectors, Patek Phillipe adds one new feature a year to its repertoire of complications.

For Patek Philippe, it is extremely rare to honor momentous occasions with the release of commemorative timepieces. To inaugurate its move to new headquarters

Above: Manually wound wristwatch with split-seconds chronograph, perpetual calendar and moon phase, ref. 5004.

Above center: Calibre 27-70/150 is composed of 404 pieces.

Right: The reference 5029 automatic chronometer with minute-repeater in an Officer-style case with hinged dust-cover. Sapphire-crystal caseback reveals the complexity of movement made of 342 parts. Total production: 10 yellow gold, 10 rose gold and 10 platinum.

never made again. The third commemorative timepiece is one of the rarest watches available today, a self-winding wrist chronometer with minute repeater. The minute repeater sounds the quarter hours, and minutes in Patek Philippe's distinctive with incomparable clarity and purity. Moving all of its operations to one location in Geneva is significant for Patek Philippe.

in 1997, Patek Philippe is introducing three wristwatch series in limited editions. The exclusive series of Pagoda men's chronometer, inspired by the design of a Chinese pagoda, have been developed. The line features a difficult to craft rectangular design that requires 73 operations to sculpt, fit and polish the case.

In all, 2,000 of the men's chronometers and 750 ladies' Pagoda watches are being produced. All of the Pagoda watches have been awarded the Geneva Seal hallmark, the official certification that every part of each watch has been produced in Geneva, the world's center of Swiss watchmaking. In fact, the men's chronometer is the first to receive the joint rating certificate, issued by the Geneva Seal Authority and the COSC (Contrôle Official Suisse des Chronometres), and the women's Pagoda has the smallest movement (calibre 16-250) ever to be hallmarked with the seal. As soon as the allotment of Pagoda watches is developed, the watchmaker will destroy all of the tools, dies and plans, ensuring the watch is

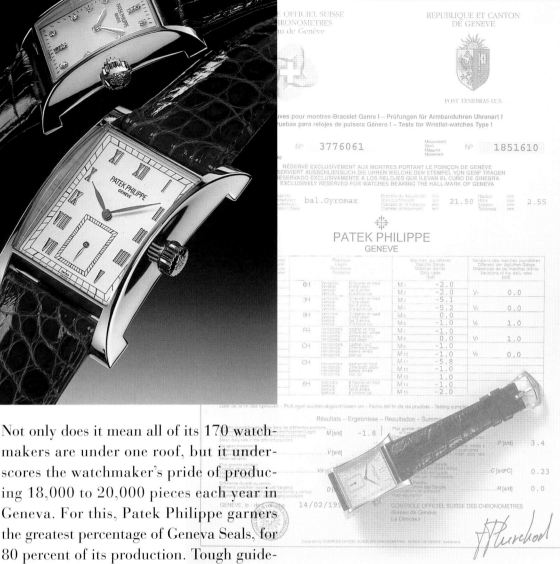

PATEK PHILIPPE
GENEVE

Not only does it mean all of its 170 watchmakers are under one roof, but it underscores the watchmaker's pride of producing 18,000 to 20,000 pieces each year in Geneva. For this, Patek Philippe garners the greatest percentage of Geneva Seals, for 80 percent of its production. Tough guidelines make it difficult for most watchmakers to qualify for the Geneva Seal, and the criteria is frequently updated to include advances in watchmaking.

Patek Philippe's move to the new headquarters is also a signal that the company continues to move forward as one of the only independent watchmakers in Geneva, and one of the few watchmakers to combine cutting-edge technology with time-honored tradition. This dynamic combination ensures that Patek Philippe's exceptional innovators will lead the watchmaking world into the new millennium, and beyond.

Above left: Pagoda watches, ref 4900 and 5500 in rose gold. The calibre 16-250 in the ladies watch is the smallest movement to be hallmarked with the Geneva Seal. A limited edition of 750 women's and 2,000 men's Pagoda watches are being produced. For the first time in watchmaking history, Switzerland's official chronometer certification bureau, the COSC (Control Officiel Suisse des Chronometres) and the Geneva Seal Authority have joined together to issue a new exclusive rating certificate. The unique certificate is specially created for Patek Philippe, in recognition of exceptional quality, precision and excellence of the watchmakers craftsmanship.

Above and below: A monumental stainless-steel sculpture by André Bucher arches 16 meters above the entrance to Patek Philippe's new watchmaking center at Plan-les-Ouates. Twin buildings house precision manufacturing and watchmaking workshops, design and engineering as well as administrative offices and archives on 37,00 square meters. The site includes a 15th and 18th century Chateau and formal garden.

Piaget

AT THE HEART of each Piaget timepiece lies the highest level of craftsmanship, the fiercest pride and ceaseless devotion to the craft — all sustained through the special bonds of ancestry. For four generations, since Georges Edouard Piaget founded the company in 1874, there has always been a member of the Piaget family shaping its legacy. Such solid heritage driving the company has allowed Piaget to embrace the sea of change that comes with time. Piaget's engineers and designers have kept ahead of the times and with every decade produced contemporary marvels — from the ultra-thin mechanical and automatic movements to Piaget's complicated watches, such as the 1997 World Premier Grande Sonnerie, one of the few of its kind in the world, a masterpiece which took two watchmakers two years to develop. And it is typical of all Piaget timepieces in that it is created by craftsmen devoted to Georges Edouard Piaget's founding pledge — to always do better than is necessary.

Previous Page: "Grande Sonnerie" Gouverneur Wristwatch. The most difficult watchmaking complication in existence: Piaget has developed a new caliber, with a 6.8 mm thickness, the smallest on the market. The chiming is at the back of the movement, behind a sapphire case back, and the hammers are on the front, so they can be seen through the dial. The watch is in 18K white gold. Only ten movements will be offered.

Bellow: The Piaget Manufacture in La Côte-aux-Fées.

Top row, left to right: Setting diamonds and rubies on the case and bracelet of a high-jewelry wristwatch; assembling of a 9P movement by a master watchmaker; Foundry: preparation of the melt of a gold ingot. Lower row, left to right: assembling of bracelet and watch of a Dancer model; checking the bracelet fitting on a watch case; mounting the components of a chain bracelet.

Bottom of page, left to right: Gouverneur "Grande Sonnerie" collection in 18K pink and white gold.

Decades before Georges Edouard Piaget officially established the Manufacture Piaget, the family was already producing watch movements in La Côte-aux-Fées, a village in the heart of the Swiss Jura. Inhabited by a serious, hard-working people, the village also enjoyed the mystical world of fairy tales. It may be that such tales, told during the dark winter nights, inspired the creative designs that Piaget would later produce. The Piaget family lived as their neighbors did in a region that grew desolate during the cold snowy winters. From November to April, the inhabitants of La Côte-aux-Fées devoted themselves to the heavily detailed work of crafting watch parts and timepieces. The family grew successful with its production of lever escapements and soon began producing entire movements.

At the turn of the century, Geneva was booming as the center for the production of timepieces, yet it wasn't until 1940 that the name Piaget would begin appearing on watches, the family having focused its business on the sales of movements. At this time, Timothée Piaget and his sons Gérald & Valentin began working to expand the

company's presence. Piaget not only began producing its own watches, but it also opened larger facilities that included a research center. It was a pivotal moment in Piaget's history. Just after World War II, top watchmakers began soliciting Piaget for even more movements. Soon afterward it was time for the third generation to lead. Gérald assumed the role of president, and with his brother Valentin at his side as vice-president, the two forged ahead with the development of the slimmest movements and timepieces. It is under their guidance that the 9P caliber came to light. The ultra-thin movement of less than 2 mm revolutionized wristwatches, in particular ladies' timepieces, whose faces Piaget widened. A steady stream of female customers discreetly thanked the watchmaker. Women no longer needed eyeglasses to see the smaller dials that had been sold to them previously. The 9P was patented in 1956, and unveiled at the 1957 fair in Basel. The family company was growing closer worldwide recognition of today, and with a newly opened boutique in Geneva, it was just a matter of time before the watchmaker became internationally renowned. Valentin spearheaded the production of other slim movements based on the 9P, and years later another landmark development cemented the watchmaker's prominence. In 1959, Piaget ushered in the world's slimmest automatic caliber, the 12P, in which the rotor of the automatic winding crown was integrated within the movement, instead of being fixed on the mechanism. At its debut, the 12P was celebrated as "an

Center left: Rectangle à l'Ancienne Men's watch in 18K yellow gold. Automatic 500P movement, gold base dial, white finish, hand guilloché center. Arabic numerals and gold hour symbols, date and center seconds. Bracelet in crocodile leather, hand sewn.

Right: The Ultra-Thin Piaget Watches. Men's models in 18K yellow or white gold, ultra-thin, automatic movement, chronometer certified, date and center seconds. Gold dial, matte white finish, four Arabic numerals or sloping Roman numerals. Crocodile leather bracelet, hand sewn.

Bottom left: "Piaget Polo" Ladies' watches, in 18K yellow gold, automatic movement, gold base dial with white matte finish, hour-symbols in gold, date and central second. On gold bracelet or leather strap.

Bottom right; Ultra-thin mechanical watches.

181

Top left: High Jewelry Minute Repeater wristwatch with "Grande Sonnerie" movement

Above left: High Jewelry Minute Repeater Wristwatch; backview.

Above right: High Jewelry Minute Repeater Wristwatch – frontview. Made in white gold. The bezel, caseband, lugs, crown and folding clasp are entirely set with baguette and trapeze-cut diamonds.

Top center and top right: Couple pocket-watches with repeater function (two photos). Based upon the fascinating Adam and Eve theme, Piaget has developed two exclusive pocket watches, a gent's and a ladies' model which, when brought together, highlight the watchmaker-jeweller art of Piaget.

Center: High Jewelry Hunting Pocket Watch, closed. Minute repeater, chronograph. Bottom right: same watch, open.

event bound to be a landmark in watch-making history." Those words certainly ring true today. Piaget's most recent exploration of the ultra-thin possibilities include an improved version of the 9P which debuted in 1996 at just 2.15 mm. A year later, Piaget released the ultra-thin automatic certified chronometer, a testimony to Piaget's exploration and dedication toward combin-

ing technical mastery with aesthetic appeal.

The first slim movements paved the way for Piaget's prosperous boom during the 1960s. The ultra-thin movements allowed greater flexibility for artistic innovation and the faces of Piaget's watches during this period reflect a boundless spirit to create. Perhaps most striking are Piaget's time-pieces with faces of precious gems that were

much sought after and sold by high-end boutiques, including Cartier and Tiffany. A watchface of mother-of-pearl made time appear as if it was floating on clouds. The simple elegance of the face, graced only with the golden hands of time and the name Piaget, was surrounded by sapphires and diamonds and white gold bands, reflecting the height of sleekness, elegance and refined taste. Piaget's designers also captured the raciness of time, with gemstones like mala-chite, turquoise, or lapis lazuli. The faces were also illustrated only by the beauty of the gemstone, the name Piaget and the hands of time. Such audacious timepieces, in rectangular or oval shapes, matched perfectly the modern styles of the era. Several enduring collections emerged, including the Protocole line which is still in production

today. Reflecting the geometric spirit of the time, the Protocole is graceful with a guilloché-style face surrounded by a rectangular bezel and clipped ends. Today, the timepiece indicates what truly a remarkable time the 1960s were for Piaget, who produced a boundless series of geometrics, bold colors and refined elegance, each and every timepiece a work of art. Piaget greeted its success through sage expansion of the realm of its craftsmanship. Piaget purchased workshops in Geneva where the company could begin producing its own bracelets and cases. Piaget now possessed complete autonomy — from the production of the

movements, to the cases and the bracelets. This sound development prepared Piaget for the rough road ahead.

The development of the quartz movement in the 1970s may have sounded the death knell for some watchmakers, but Piaget took a practical approach on the sound advice of the newest member of the family and the leader of the fourth generation, Yves Piaget. Fresh from his travels abroad, Yves Piaget had completed his studies in watchmaking and gemology. When his father consulted Yves about the quartz development, the youngest member of the firm advised Piaget to join in the production of quartz movements but without sacrificing the development of its renowned mechanical movements. Even then, Yves Piaget understood that the innovation would not supersede both the precision of hand-crafted timepieces and man's appreciation for such items. In keeping with tradition, Piaget's engineers developed the world's thinnest quartz movement. But it is clear that the heart of Piaget beats with a mechanical movement. Today, Piaget is enjoying noteworthy worldwide success. Such expansion is owed to the spirit of Yves

Above: "Grande Sonnerie" High Jewelry Pocket Watch. Ornamented with diamonds, emeralds and mother-of-pearl.

Top left: "Protocole" chronograph, 18K yellow gold.

Top center: "Protocole" on gold bracelet, men's watch in 18K white gold, mechanical hour-minute movement, bezel and dial in guilloché gold.

Below left: "Protocole" men's and ladies' models in 18K white gold.

Clockwise from top left: "Rectangle à l'ancienne" collection in 18K white, yellow, and pink gold, in a variety of dial finishes: black matte with transfer white Arabic numerals; silvered satin-finish with Roman hour-markers, polished in old-time style; gold color; pink gold finish with Arabic numerals.

Below: "Rectangle à l'ancienne" watch with secret case-back, entirely decorated by hand. Piaget 9P2 movement.

Piaget, who assumed a role as ambassador for the watchmaker. Yves Piaget realized that the humble producer of magnificent watches needed a worldwide scope, and he began traveling the continents to show. The result is that Piaget watches are available around the world, in 10 boutiques, the newest having recently opened in New York, 70 Espaces Piaget across five continents or at selected retailers around the globe. With

an eye on the future, Yves Piaget in the 1980s began steering the watchmaker toward the development of complications. It proved an astute business move, connoisseurs and collectors showing renewed interest in complications soon afterwards.

Piaget continues its evolution today. By forging ahead with the Vendôme Group in 1988, Piaget renewed its commitment to the European market, as well as the develop-

ment of high-end luxury goods. Already a success in America and the Far East, Piaget also manufactures refined, elegant timepieces sought after by Europeans. Among the new developments are the classic Rectangle à l'ancienne and Citéa lines of timepieces.

As always, Piaget advances the development of the slimmest watch movements. The new generation includes the innovative 500P and 430P automatic and manually wound movements. The new movements undergo the most rigorous testing, ensuring that the timepieces housing them will rise in value as they are passed down from generation to generation.

From the very beginning, the Piaget family has been deliberate in its goals to create top-of-the-range timepieces, produced only in gold or platinum, that live up to the dual standards of luxury and precision. For four generations the watchmaker has quietly done so, much to the amazement of leaders in the watchmaking industry. And it is certainly living up to its credo that "Piaget time is measured only in gold."

Robergé

HIGHLY COMPLEX, 100 percent Swiss-made wristwatches, whose innovative style and refinement of detail in the pure tradition of watchmaking succeed in reflecting the mysterious beauty of the stars whose names they have borrowed - Andromède, Castor, Pegase, M31... The Robergé wristwatch collection was shown for the first time ever at the International Watch and Jewelry Show in 1997 in Basel, Switzerland, in the hall traditionally reserved for the most prestigious brands. Acclaimed by the general public and professionals alike, Robergé's success was the fruit of 16 months of relentless effort to spark growth for a make already recognized among connoisseurs for 25 years. In a record time of eight months, Robergé's designers created 60 models grouped in five distinct collections. With the creation in 1995 of a watchmaking firm fitted with the finest in technical and human resources, Robergé has the instruments essential to wider recognition.

Above: Andromède II Minute Repeater Tourbillon in 18K pink gold. Both the tourbillon and the minute repeater represent extremely complex horological devices, requiring virtuoso talent. Reflecting the painstaking finish of the mechanism, the watch is adorned with a hand-engraved dial. The beating heart of this watchmaking marvel, visible through the sapphire case-back which also reveals the dance of the tourbillon, is enhanced by finely hand-engraved motifs.

Below: Andromède II Minute Repeater watches in 18K white gold chime the hours in a truly distinguished manner. The Roman numerals and gold hands on a background which is delicately hand-engraved on a rose engine, bear discreet witness to the classical refinement of genuine craftsmanship. Coiled up within the case, two gongs await the strike of two tiny chiming hammers which melodiously chime the hours, quarters and minutes against their delicate steel spirals.

In 1890, in his native city of Beirut, David Mouawad founded a dynasty that would gain international renown by setting up shop as a watchmaker-jeweler. Yet it was not until 82 years later, when his grandson took over the reins of the family business, that the powerful Mouawad Group would relocate to Geneva and seal the name of Robergé — a contraction of Robert Mouawad's name and Geneva — as the sacred union of jewelry and prestige watchmaking.

In an audacious move, Alain Mouawad, Robert's son, decided to establish his family's firm in the Swiss cradle of traditional watchmaking, and to entrust the reins of the company to Jean-Daniel Dubois, one of the most talented watchmakers in the Vallée de Joux, who has made numerous, patented contributions to his art. Since November 1995, in the village of Le Brassus, a close-knit team of engineers and seasoned artisans have been tracking the secrets of time in order to offer an exacting clientele wristwatches that are worthy of the mysterious intergalactic works guiding their inspiration.

Above center: Diamond-studded Andromède II Tourbillon joaillerie in 18K white gold. A particularly spectacular feature of this version of Andromède II Complication lies in the generous space reserved on the dial side for the tourbillon carriage whose larger than average size optimises its level of performance. The distinctive dial has been reduced, off-centered and diamond-studded to underscore the harmony of this original watch face.

Right: Manufacture of watches Robergé at "Le Brassus".

A love for beautiful watch mechanisms — which are as rare and precious as the extraordinary gems gathered by Robert Mouawad — prompted Robergé to adopt an uncompromising ethic in which production is subjected to rigorous quality control. In order to ensure the complete mastery of watchmaking down to the most minute of details, the Le Brassus-based Manufacture is fostering a three-phase development strategy to begin designing and producing its own automatic movements, then producing its own cases and metal bracelets.

Presently a staff of 17, working in the former Breguet factory, ensure precision in the assembling of watch components, case included, which have been acquired exclusively from renowned Swiss suppliers. It is the absolute and unfailing wish of the house to offer only 100 percent Swiss products; it is this drive for supreme

Below: The three RS models. A dynamic sporting interpretation of the founding Andromède design, available in three automatic models: Andromède RS Automatic, Andromède Regulator, Andromède RS Power Reserve. Polished steel case, water-resistant to 30 meters. Screw-down crown, Double-face convex glareproofed glass. Light-green tritium-coated Roman numerals, pointers and hands. Hand-stitched sharkskin Connoly strap.

quality that is proudly guaranteed by the label "Manufacturé en Suisse," chosen over the all too common Swiss Made designation.

This return to traditional language is more than symbolic. It underlines an attention to detail seen in the case, which visibly expresses the functioning excellence of the movement. At Robergé, subtle elements reveal the scrupulous attention given to the finishing touches. This is seen in the double-sealed crown, screwed-down back and the convex glareproof sapphire crystal through which the secret signature of the brand appears: the R that, whether encircled or not, personalizes the crown.

But beyond such brand distinction, the aesthetic appeal of Robergé watches is also characterized by the fluidity of lines, the originality of colors and shapes,

Three Castor models.
Top center and below: Robergé celebrates the Gemini constellation with a classically inspired watch, featuring a painstaking finish in harmony with the noblest watchmaking tradition, its bevelled bezel, mother-of-pearl engraved dial, fluted lugs and the special blanked out overdial segment with a Clous de Paris decorative pattern, give a definite aura of originality to this high-tech collection of timekeepers, comprising a COSC* certified chronometer with three-day power reserve. *Swiss Official Chronometer Testing Agency

Center: Perpetual Calendar with transparent case-back, yellow or white gold, or steel

the finesse of the guilloché work, the meticulousness of the hand-engraving on the oscillating weight of certain movements. In short, it is the blending of the most ancient savoir-faire and the most advanced techniques to imprint upon metals a treatment that matches their nobility.

This vocation for excellence no doubt allows the contemporary style of Robergé watches to approach the immortality of the constellations whose names they are honoring. They are fitted with a range of movements — automatic, mecha-electronic and, more rarely, quartz — as solidly and painstakingly crafted as the cases that enclose them. It is a quest for timelessness of which the founder of the Mouawad dynasty would have approved — he was, after all, a man who spent 50 years repairing and ensuring long life for church clocks.

However, it was his grandson Robert who began producing collections, in complement to one-of-a-kind pieces, and inspired the Robergé style with the first Andromède collection. Its case shape is simultaneously so original and universal that it is already considered a classic. Its mysterious design, blending the circle, oval and ellipse — without being defined as more one shape

than the other — has remained inextricably linked to the image of the brand and serves as its signature. As the Robergé flagship collection for a quarter of a century, the Andromède prototype has given birth to a surprising number of variations now streamlined into two collections: Andromède II and Andromède RS. In the image of the initial model, the collections that spring forth opt for a dynamic style and a resolutely contemporary, sporty elegance.

Under the name of Andromède RS, three automatic models with high-precision balance feature silvered dials and brushed silver hour-circles in soft gradations of gray, nuances of lime-green tritium in the hands, and a generous bezel in polished steel prolonged by rectilinear horns. There is a simple version with day, date and second in the center; a Regulateur version with an auxiliary hour dial, day hand and second hand, and finally a time reserve version, with reserve indicator.

Inspired by the scintillating contours of the only spiral nebula visible to the naked eye, Andromède II adds four new stars to the firmament of fine watchmaking: a Chronometer, a Double Reserve de Marche (power reserve), a Chronograph and a Quantieme Perpetuel, in yellow and white gold, steel, and upon request, platinum. The

Above: Andromède Perpetual Calendar. The layout of the dial of the steel Andromède II Quantieme perpétual (above) reflects the fundamental originality of the specially shaped case favoured by Robergé. In addition to the automatic movement, a perpetual calendar mechanism displays the date, month, day of the week, leap-year cycle and moon phases on four subdials.

Left: Innovation is still the keynote in this yellow gold Andromède II a double power reserve, the dial of which features two fan-shaped indicators displaying in blue the level of energy remaining in its double-barrel automatic mechanism. Also available in steel.

Left: M31 Power Reserve in 18K white gold, pink gold dial, tritium-coated pointers

Near Left: M31 three-day power reserve in 18K yellow gold, porcelain dial, glass caseback.

Below: Andromède II Chronographe in 18K gray gold. Mecha-electronic movement, double-sealed crown. Water-resistant to 30 meters. Porcelain dial.

sophistication of the movements is mirrored in the dials, whose distinction is tinged with originality, shown in the rose gold guilloché work, silver or slate-gray hour-circles and the particular fan-shaped configuration of the two reserve indicators. An innovative design with central fastenings and soft lines that matches both sporty and classic watch dials, made substantive by the chronograph's large push-buttons.

But without a doubt it is the M31, a new kind of sports watch, that enjoys the greatest amount of freedom in the theme of innovation. From the Automatique 3 Jours model to the Réserve de Marche and Chronograph, this series' virile elegance is endowed progressively with audacious color contrasts, breathing a very contemporary dynamism into the classic ideal of a round wristwatch, in steel, yellow gold or 18K white gold.

Dedicated to the poetic inspiration symbolized by the mythical winged-steed Pegasus, Pegase rattles convention with an original case, whose shape hovers between a square and a rectangle. This is a watch with great stylistic purity and its slightly larger dimensions enable the observer to admire the quality of its details.

The equally well-crafted Castor line draws its inspiration from the highest watchmaking tradition to offer a classic aesthetic elegance with a discreetly contemporary touch. The collection pays refined homage to the mythological figure who was transformed into a constellation. Double-fluted curved horns, a beveled bezel and a case decorated with an unusual stamped Clous de Paris motif characterize this round watch, available in two models. The first is a double-barrel Chronometer with a high-precision 72-hour automatic movement; the

Right: Two Pégase models. The winged horse of mythology transformed into a constellation. Pegasus inspired Robergé to create an original ladies watch, its slightly larger than average dimensions display the distinctive signs of exceptional craftsmanship: screw-down winding crown engraved with an R, glareproofed glass, carefully designed dials with date display at 4.30. They also give scope for the most artistic embellishments using gem-setting and hand-engraving techniques. Available in pink, yellow or white 18K gold on leather strap. Electronic movement.

Left: Andromède II Chronograph. Finely engraved on the caseback of all Robergé watches are the 18K gold disc embossed with the R logo, along with the name and personal identification number of the watch, and the words "Manufacturé en Suisse," replacing the overworked and thus devalued "Swiss made" label.

Push-piece on the Andromède II Chronograph. Underscoring the subtle outlines of its trapeze-shaped push-pieces with rounded angles, meticulous stamping and polishing idealises the contemporary purity of the Chronographe Andromède II.

Transparent caseback of the M31 Power-Reserve. Hand-engraved on a rose engine into the 21K oscillating weight of the M31 Power Reserve, the sunray motif so dear to Robergé requires a degree of mastery rare among engravers today. A sapphire glass integrated within the screw-down case back provides a clear view of this refined craftsmanship.

second a Quantieme Perpetuel day watch with a transparent sapphire crystal back revealing the intricate movement.

Such devotion for technical and aesthetic excellence is demonstrated by other chefs-d'oeuvres. Through its Grandes Complications, Tourbillon, Repetition Minutes and the supreme prowess of Répétition Minutes Tourbillon, Andromède II ascends to the highest spheres of watchmaking art. Its case slightly fills out to incorporate the complications. Traditional decoration techniques, such as diamond-pavé, hand-engraved guillochage and the application of natural mother-of-

Right: Andromède II for ladies comes in a more feminine size, without losing the details which are an integral part of its charm, 18K yellow gold case, water-resistant to 30 meters, on hand-stitched Louisiana crocodile strap. Double sealed winding-crown. Sapphire crystal case-back. Silvered dial with velvet-effect centre and satin-brushed hour-circle. Date display at 6 o'clock.

Left: Another exclusive Robergé feature is the seconds hand extended by a personalized R counterweight. It goes on turning while the luminous "reed" hour and minute hands of the Andromède RS move over the engraved dial.

pearl, together offer the watch an eminently original dial in which the hours, shown in a miniaturized auxiliary dial, reserve the spotlight for the whirling dance of the tourbillon, visible through a sapphire crystal.

Robergé reveals its spirit of independence in the creation of special, unique models in the Grandes Complications series. The "Naja" Tourbillon in 18K white gold showcases a rose gold appliqué of a sacred animal on a red coral dial. Located over the escapement, the image appears once again on the back of the watch, engraved in a master's hand in the nickel silver plate. Just as astonishing is the "Heron" Répétition Minutes, which inaugurates a series of exceptional naturalist pieces: engraved in 18K gold on the dial, the

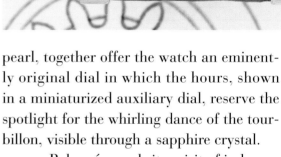

animal is surprised in its natural habitat while a glass back reveals a bouquet of hand-engraved reeds.

The Manufacture des Montres Robergé ventures into 20th century art with the Cubisme Chronometre. This watch, liberated from convention, was entrusted to today's most talented artists, who engraved the mechanism with a savvy composition. The geometric shapes reproduce the dynamics of light and among the rays nestles the R of Robergé.

The R logo, the center of a radiance that is open to the infinite, is the symbol of a promise of "supreme quality" made by Alain Mouawad and Jean-Daniel Dubois on November 13, 1995, the day the Manufacture was inaugurated. The oath ensures Robergé's rapid ascension to the summit of watchmaking, so that it might figure among the 10 great international brands. The term 'rapid' is a manner of speaking for men who limited their 1997 production to 3,500 watches (each emblazoned with a personal number), and who know that time, the essential raw material of their art, demands to be treated with the utmost care. "Above all, we did not wish to step on the accelerator, in particular when it comes to quality control... We have taken this direction in the company with precisely the ambition of mastering all the parameters in order to offer a product that is above reproach. To do so, we will spend all the time that is needed."

The immediate and resounding success of Robergé's new collections worldwide is testimony that the watchmaker has swiftly stepped up to take its place among the great names of Swiss watchmaking. Present in the five zones of the international market as of 1998, the brand has taken all the measures necessary to the development of a selective distribution network in harmony with its exclusive constellations of models: timekeeping pieces of high technical quality and featuring refined contemporary elegance.

Vacheron Constantin

THAT THE WORLD'S oldest watchmaker remains today one of the best says as much about the watchmaking tradition as it does about the company itself, Vacheron Constantin. Founded in 1755, Jean-Marc Vacheron was one of hundreds pursuing the horological craft in Geneva. Known as a "cabinotier," because of the brightly lit attic spaces, or cabinets, where master watchmakers crafted highly detailed timepieces, Vacheron worked diligently to create the most precise time-keeping mechanisms. With the help of his sons Louis Andre and Abraham, the business gained notoriety, and this was honored by succeeding heirs, who tapped talented and specialized craftsman to secure the watchmaker's status. In 1819, the affable, enterprising François Constantin led Vacheron's expansion across Europe, building up a sturdy list of new clients while cementing relationships with the old. In no time, he would join forces with Constantin, forever changing the watchmaker's name. It was Constantin who exacted perfection from each watchmaker with his motto, "Do better if possible... and that's always possible."

Previous page: Women's and men's wristwatches in 18K gold from Vacheron Constantin's most recent collection, Overseas. Both feature a round case fitted with a scratch resistant sapphire crystal protecting a silvered, engine-turned dial with sweep seconds hand and date calendar at 3 o'clock (for men). Self-winding mechanical movements with rotor rimmed in gold. Men's version is a certified Royal Chronometer whose bracelet features a double safety catch. Water resistant to 150 meters.

Below: From Les Complications collection. Round platinum case with a sapphire crystal and a transparent back reveals an open-worked, skeleton type self-winding mechanical movement with a perpetual calendar showing the date, the day of the week, the month and the phases of the moon.

Top center: One of the most challenging designs that classic watchmaking has to offer, this skeleton tourbillon from the Les Complications family features a movement with twin series-coupled barrels. Its regulating unit, escapement and balance wheel, are mounted in a tourbillon carriage that rotates on itself over one minute. Skeletonizing required removing more than 71 percent of the movement's original metal before housing it in an 18K rose gold case. In addition to a few open worked specimens, only 300 Tourbillons will be produced.

Top right: This classic masterpiece of watchmaking, in the grand tradition of the "Les Complications" family, features a hand-wound mechanical movement encased in 18K rose gold that is the exact replica of one of its proprietary calibers from the 1930s and still, at 3.28 mm, the thinnest of its kind made today. It strikes on demand the hours, quarters and minutes. Production of all minute repeaters is strictly limited to 200.

Constantin's personality and superb public relations skills allowed him to charm his way into the best salons of Europe and beyond. As a result, Vacheron was commissioned to create the most exquisite horological creations for dukes, counts, princes and ambassadors in all of the palaces of Europe. In the early 19th century, Europe found herself in the throes of post-revolutionary decadence. The pursuit of luxury and leisure among the aristocracy suddenly became incredibly fashionable. Vacheron Constantin became the ultimate company to supply the ultimate accessory, the watch, and its distribution grew as far away as Rio de Janeiro, Stockholm, Malta, Liverpool, the United States, the Far East and Russia.

In 1839, the addition of Georges-Auguste Leschot would seal Vacheron Constantin's predominance in the watch-making industry. Vacheron and Constantin invited him to join the company with the challenge to mechanically manufacture the components of their watches. A mechanical

genius, Leschot invented equipment to produce watch parts and in less than two years, Leschot built a range of machines capable of turning out any watch part in any size and perfectly adapted to the existing calibers. This revolutionized the watchmaking world and enabled Vacheron Constantin to develop its watchmaking expertise, producing increasingly sophisticated designs and complicated timepieces. Increasingly accurate metal fabrication and milling technology enabled watchmakers to create complex, precise complications, including the moon phase indicator, a full calendar, to the split-second chronograph and the tourbillon. Advancements also burst forth in the realm of creativity. Artisans began exploring both style and decoration, eagerly applying their growing experience and expertise to ever more challenging designs. During this time the intrinsically detailed artwork of enameling began appearing on timepieces.

In 1880, Vacheron Constantin adopted as its symbol the Maltese Cross — the small toothed wheel which adjusted the tension of the spring in old watches. For over 100 years the creations of Vacheron Constantin have borne this symbol, demonstrating the watchmaker's attachment to the

Top: Vacheron Constantin S.A., Geneva, Switzerland. In addition to housing the historic corporation, located here is the Vacheron Constantin Museum, consisting of over 400 models collected over two centuries, including the first pocket watch hand-crafted by founder Jean Marc Vacheron in 1735. On the ground floor is the Vacheron Constantin store where the current watch lines and designer jewelry can be seen on display.

Top left: Men's 18K gold skeleton watch from Les Complications line. Sixteen-sided bezel is enhanced with .56 carats diamonds. Extra-thin self-winding movement decorated by hand. Gold bridges are hand-engraved and finished.

Bottom left: Men's platinum Perpetual Calendar Chronograph on a crocodile strap from Les Complications line. Its self-winding mechanical movement includes a 12-hour and 30-minute totalizer along with an auxiliary plate for a perpetual calendar mechanism that shows the day, date and month, automatically adjusting for months with 28, 29, 30 or 31 days, along with the phases of the moon. The moon phase indicator doubles as a subdial for the seconds. Chronograph timing operations and all adjustments and corrections effected by two push pieces and four correctors on the rim of the case. Dial plate in engine-turned 18K gold with applied gold hour markers and studs.

Top: Open-faced pocket watches in 18K yellow gold from Les Historiques collection. Fitted with a secret catch, their coverlids are enameled in the finest tradition of Geneva, featuring views of Geneva taken from 18th century prints.

Right: Men's strap watch from the Les Complications collection inspired by Vacheron Constantin's 240th Anniversary watch. Encased in 18K white gold with a self-winding mechanical movement. The silvered, engine-turned dial features a circular date calendar between 2 and 3, a seconds subdial at 6 and power reserve indicator between 10 and 11.

Far right: Perpetual Calendar Minute Repeater from "Les Complications" family faithfully replicates a design from the late 1930s. It contains an amazingly thin hand wound mechanical movement measuring only 3.3 mm. It strikes on demand hours, quarters, minutes. Its perpetual calendar shows the day, date and month, automatically adjusting for months with 28, 29, 30 or 31 days, along with the phases of the moon. Featured in 18K yellow gold with a silvered dial bearing hour markers and studs. Including all model variants, production of Vacheron Constantin minute repeaters is limited to 200 in all.

Cabinotiers' values, instruments and ideas. To this day, Vacheron Constantin honors the strength of its watchmaking roots. On display in the company's private museum in Geneva — among 400 other timepieces — is the first recorded timepiece ever created by Jean-Marc Vacheron.

Today, Vacheron Constantin excels in its production of five collections —

of classic timepieces, the Overseas collection marks the watchmaker as resolutely modern. Designed in steel worked and finished in the manner of platinum, Overseas is an impressive entry into the development of sports watches.

The Les Complications timepieces are among the most celebrated at Vacheron Constantin, from minute repeaters to per-

Overseas, Les Historiques, Les Joailleries, Les Essentielles and Les Complications. Every single watch is created in observance of long-standing tradition, and in strictly limited series. By retaining such rigorous control, Vacheron Constantin is sure to please each owner of its timepieces.

While Vacheron Constantin will always be known as a master in its creation

petual calendars to the tourbillon, they provide a canvas for innovation and embody the most impressive traditions in watchmaking. At the top of Les Complications collection is the Grande Complication watch, with more than 500 components and no less than 15 functions. It features a chronograph mechanism, a perpetual calendar fitted on an additional movement plate along with a

Left: John James Audubon's "Birds of America," published toward the middle of the last century, inspired the limited-edition series of timepieces. Each dial features a champlevé-enamel reproduction of one of Audubon's illustrations of a native American bird. The enameling is the work of Mrs. Muriel Sechaud of Geneva, an unusually talented practitioner of the centuries-old, Genevan specialty. Featuring the long-billed curlew, the dial is framed in an 18K yellow gold case with a back cover lid opened by pressing a hidden spring catch called a secret to reveal its self-winding mechanical movement.

minute repeater, a 12-hour and 30-hour totalizer. It also possesses a highly-advanced calendar which shows the day of the week, the month, date and the phases of the moon. Encased in solid gold, only 3 masteries were created. Yet the same attention to detail and technical expertise that went into developing the Grande Complication is bestowed upon every single timepiece created at Vacheron

Constantin, and incomparable seal of quality in the watchmaking world.

Sharing the spotlight in the world of complications is one of the most challenging designs, the Skeleton Tourbillon. In order to create the skeleton, engineers removed 71 percent of the movements original metal before housing it in a rose gold case. The tourbillon movement can be seen through a frame of artwork. In addition to a few open worked specimens, only 300 will be produced.

Always masterful at reproducing its antique timepieces, Vacheron Constantin presents the Skeleton Minute Repeater, a

Above: Mercator. Inspired by the founder of modern cartography, Gerardus Mercator, this timepiece features a choice of hand-chased dials with a map of the Americas or Europe, Asia and Africa. The hour and minute hands are fitted on an off-centered axis and move over two graduated sectors in a retrograde time-display system.

Far left: From Les Complications line, this self-winding wristwatch displays a simple calendar: the day, date, week and phases of the moon. While the hour and minute hands provide the precise time, the week is shown by a crescent tipped pointer sweeping around the dial. The day and date are provided by a pair of subdials and a rotating disc shows the phases of the moon.

Below: Special edition Jalousie is strictly limited to 125. Its originality lies in a unique system of 18K white gold engraved shutters which cover the dial and can be opened and closed with a small slide piece set with a sapphire cabochon. Its rectangular waterproof case is in 18K pink gold with engraved roman numerals on the bezel. Each is fitted with a hand-wound mechanical movement with a subdial for the seconds at 6. In keeping with its strong character, these highly unusual timepieces come with a white dial with blue steel hand and gold hour markers.

Right: Fiorenza. Women's gems set watches from Les Joailleries line. Crescent moon style bracelets in 18K white gold are each set with 454 diamonds totaling 5.08 carats. The square-shaped face is covered with 110 pavé diamonds, the oval-shaped case, 106 pavé diamonds. Quartz movement.

Bottom: Seal of Geneva. Timepiece from Les Historiques collection features a trim 18K yellow gold case with transparent back, showcasing the meticulous care and patience with which every component of its self-winding movement has been designed and made, then delicately finished in contrasting matte and polished areas.

classic masterpiece in the grand tradition, featuring a hand-wound mechanical movement that is the exact replica of one of its proprietary calibers from the 1930s and still, at 3.28 mm, the thinnest of its kind made today. It strikes on demand hours, quarters, minutes. Much like the Skeleton Tourbillon, engineers had to remove much of the case, more than half, to create the skeleton.

The rare practice of enameling, typical to Geneva, is explored at Vacheron Constantin through the impressive John James Audubon series. Although the artistic endeavor is dwindling in practice today, Vacheron Constantin continues to explore its possibilities, and has tapped Geneva's most talented artist, Muriel Séchaud, to recreate the splendor of Audubon's, "Birds of America," published toward the middle of the last century. On each dial is a marvelous champlevé-enamel reproduction of one of Audubon's illustrations of a native American bird.

Vacheron Constantin is renowned for such forays into history, and frequently delves into its own horological archives. The watchmaker's Les Historiques collection features the best of Vacheron Constantin, the most successful designs produced in recent years are reissued, much to the delight of collectors and connoisseurs. In homage to early watchmaking, two pocket watches boast enamel recreations, by Séchaud, of views of the Geneva area taken from an 18th-century print. In the Seal of Geneva timepiece, a transparent case back reveals the movements Seal of Geneva, applied exclusively by watchmakers and manufacturers established in the canton of Geneva.

Intricate jewels and delicate detail illuminate the Les Joailleries collection. Through the use of the most precious of metals, luminous

erty together in homage to the Italian Renaissance.

Each collection underscores François Constantin's pursuit of excellence, and every timepiece is built with the skills and expertise accumulated over nearly two and a half decades. Such wealth of knowledge is formidable in the world of watchmaking, built slowly and steadily with utmost determination and dedication through the generations at Vacheron Constantin.

Most recently, the watchmaker has joined the prestigious Vendôme Group, ensuring its leading place in the world of luxury watchmaking. The watchmaker is also committed at every level, from its craftsmen to its sales representatives, to communicate the esteem and ethics that the company extols as it develops incomparable watches. Just as Vacheron Constantin's timepieces have always reflected the splendor of the times, it is certain they will continue to delight and increase in value with the next generations.

platinum, white and yellow gold, the most precious of gems will be showcased for eternity. The collections include Kalla, inspired by the Kallista (the world's most costly time-piece), and Fiorenza, the latter dedicated to the sensitivity of today's woman. With flawless diamonds, glowing, deep-hued rubies and sapphires set in lustrous white or yellow gold, the "Fiorenza" collection salutes woman and lib-

Top Left: Responding to the demands of ever more discerning consumers intrigued by the period styles, the company's designers and watchmakers have revisited a Vacheron Constantin model dating from 1912 made to fit men and women alike. Silvered by the traditional process, the dial features stylized numerals in pure turn-of-the-century fashion dancing elegantly around the dial. Under it beats a hand-wound mechanical movement, exactly as in 1912. This individually numbered reissue of the Vacheron Constantin "1912" is limited to a total of 1912 pieces: 1412 in pink gold and 500 in white gold.

Left: Historique. Men's 18K yellow gold strap watch from Les Historiques collection. Rectangular case features a manual movement. The silvered engine-turned dial with three roman numeral and 9 triangular applied gold markers displays a sub-second dial at 6.

Van Cleef & Arpels

JUST AFTER THE TURN of the century, four young men began a celebrated journey into the world of jewelry and watches, making a name for themselves that became synonymous with elegance and building a solid reputation as a leader among the world's great jewelers. In 1906, Alfred Van Cleef formed a partnership with his brothers-in-law, Julien, Louis and Charles Arpels. All four were practicing jewelers and diamond cutters at the time. The men established a boutique in the stylish Place Vendôme, frequented by wealthy tourists drawn to Paris as the only place to replenish wardrobes and also drawn to the historic and beautiful square by the newly-opened Ritz Hotel. Van Cleef & Arpels flourished during this time of celebrated wealth, as Europe displayed the riches of the good life by wearing and purchasing gifts of jewelry.

Previous page: The newest Signature
timepiece in white gold with three rows of
diamonds surrounding the bezel. Three rows
of diamonds are also woven around one of
the bracelet links.

Above: "P.A. 49" gents' watch in 18K yellow
gold. LC extra-flat manual movement. Water-
resistant watch also available with an ETA
quartz movement.

Top center: Roma. The large stainless steel
bezel encases the black dial with white
numeric accents and sweep second hand.

Van Cleef & Arpels quickly assumed prestige with their flawless knowledge of precious stones. Exclusive boutiques were opened along the Coast of France in Cannes, Deauville and Monte Carlo—as well as the spa resort Vichy—before successfully establishing a boutique on Fifth Avenue in New York City, followed by Palm Beach and Beverly Hills.

A grateful client once said, "There are signatures that we treasure." That is certainly true today as Van Cleef & Arpels launches its newest Signature timepiece.

A strong interwoven link bracelet gracefully blends an elegant piece of jewelry into a precision watch. Gleaming in variations of pink, white and yellow gold, this new signature timepiece radiates when enhanced by a diamond bezel — and ultimately — with diamond encrusted links.

Each watch gracefully bears the exquisite and exclusive prestige of one of the world's most famous jewelers and its glorious history. As with every item of jewelry, the watches are flawlessly breathtaking creations of elegance. Tasteful, aesthetic form is combined with luxurious materials. This watch is for the woman of today who treasures the architectural richness of design history which only Van Cleef & Arpels can offer its clients.

P.A. 49

It was the simple geometric union of a straight line intersecting a circle that laid the basis for Van Cleef & Arpels' extraordinary success, the P.A. 49 timepiece. Deciding he wanted his very own watch, Pierre Arpels set out one fine July day in 1949 to design the timepiece of his dreams. The result is an absolutely flat watch face, connected to the wristband by two studs, one at 12 and another at 6, both at the center of an axis. The band covers all but the center stud and two studs capping the edge of the axis, creating an elegant, delicate timepiece.

Unable to keep his watch a secret from admiring customers and friends, Pierre Arpels was repeatedly sought after by those who wanted a P.A. 49 watch of their own. In no time, the concept inspired an entire collection, each timepiece retaining the central fastening point. Even as Van Cleef & Arpels opened its "Boutique des Heures" devoted to watches in 1972, the P.A. 49 still enjoyed celebrity status among the many variations. The stylish simplicity of the P.A. 49 remains the foundation for the watches of today — elegant interpretations that carry on the destiny of Van Cleef & Arpels most famous timepiece.

Below, top to bottom: "Classique" ladies watch in 18K yellow gold. Case with one row of 57 diamonds (0.5 carats) and dial paved with 186 diamonds (0.77 carats). Bracelet in 18K yellow gold with 294 (2.54 carats). Water resistant. "Classique" ladies watch in 18K yellow gold. Case with one row of 57 diamonds (0.5 carats) and bracelet in 18K yellow gold with 120 (1.14 carats). Water resistant. "Classique" ladies' watch. Case and bracelet in 18K yellow gold. Water-resistant.

Roma. Eternal City - Eternal Style

Paris. Rome. Two names to conjure with. Two cultures underpinning the whole edifice of the modern world. Two artistic traditions which Van Cleef & Arpels, the celebrated jewelers of the Place Vendôme have married in their watch collection: Roma.

The jewelers from Paris, steeped in their own artistic tradition, have been to the waters of the Tiber to draw inspiration for a watch of a rare design. With its imposing case extended by generous attachments and with its broad bezel of polished gold or matte-finished steel, Roma embodies the sense of balance and proportion of a rediscovered classicism. As individual as it is contemporary, as varied in detail as it is unified in design, this athletic collection is already marked out as a classic for the new millennium. A black or white lacquer face, Arabic or Roman numerals, metal or leather strap with normal or deployment buckle, automatic movement (for men only) or quartz: this wealth of choice symbolizes the creative riches of the Eternal City.

"Mini-Carrée" ladies' watch in 18K yellow gold. Case with two rows of 89 diamonds (0.73 carats) and bracelet in 18K yellow gold with 152 diamonds (1.46 carats).

"Mini-Carrée" ladies' watch in 18K yellow gold. Case with two rows of 89 diamonds (0.73 carats), dial with 80 diamonds (0.30 carats) and bracelet in 18K yellow gold with 294 diamonds (2.54 carats).

"Mini-Carrée" ladies' watch in 18K yellow gold. Case with two rows of 89 diamonds (0.73 carats) and green lizard strap with 18K yellow gold buckle.

"Fantasy" ladies' watch in 18K yellow gold. Case with two rows of 81 diamonds (0.76 carats). Inter-changeable bracelet in 18K yellow gold and blue lizard strap with a yellow gold-plated buckle.

Classique and Fantasy collections

The Classique collection illustrates Van Cleef & Arpels' tradition of elegance to perfection, revered by connoisseurs and collectors alike. The case for the quartz movement is kept slim, allowing the watch to retain the sleek and sophisticated shape that is once again stirring passions worldwide, as it is a modern interpretation of the traditional P.A. 49.

This design is also offered in the smaller format known as the mini-carrée watch. Worn subtly on the wrist, the mini-carrée are truly diminutive treasures that are testimony to the maxim that luxury is not, and never will be, conspicuous.

An enduring level of sophistication is also offered in the Fantasy watch. The collection of ladies watches is a treasure of elegant timepieces ranging from the more modest gold to completely covered in diamond pavé

Right: "1930" jewelry mini-ladies' watch. Case in 18K yellow gold set with 68 diamonds (0.50 carats), attachments with 60 diamonds (0.30 carats) and two round cabochon emeralds (0.28 carats). Buckle in 18K yellow gold with green moiré strap.

Far right: "1930" jewelry mini-ladies' watch. Case in 18K yellow gold set with 60 diamonds (0.55 carats), attachments with 32 diamonds (0.27 carats) and two round cabochon sapphires (0.40 carats). Buckle in 18K yellow gold with blue moiré strap.

Below: "1930" jewelry mini-ladies' watch. Case in 18K yellow gold set with 74 diamonds (0.45 carats), attachments with 40 diamonds (0.41 carats) and two round cabochon rubies (0.42 carats). Buckle in 18K yellow gold with yellow moiré strap.

designs. The jeweler is renowned for extolling the beauty of a woman, a tradition that perseveres through the refined style of the Fantasy watch with its interchangeable pearl and gold bracelet, accompanied by a menagerie of colorful crocodile, lizard and satin straps.

The history of the Fantasy watch dates back to a famous client of the House who could not find enough hours in the day. "Monsieur" she began, "I rarely find time in the evening to change for the opera. I would at least like to have a watch which can be conveniently converted from a day model to a timepiece for festive occasions."

Intrigued by the concept, and ever attentive to the needs of the client, Jacques Arpels set out to create the Fantasy watch, based on the classic watch, but with interchangeable bands that make the transition between different spheres of life effortless. In a unique and secure system, the band is easily removed to suit the occasion.

The 1930 collection

The day Van Cleef & Arpels established their salon at 22 Place Vendôme, its jewels began drawing the attention of nobility and film legends, and, of course, making an impact on jewelry in France. Numerous exhibits through the 1920s celebrated the young jeweler, and Van Cleef & Arpels reaped top awards at the leading exhibitions of the time.

In a reverent bow to its own history, the jeweler is drawing from the era that firmly established it as a prestigious jeweler and the woman credited with its graceful creations during the 30s. Inspired by the work of Renée Puissant, daughter of co-founder Alfred Van Cleef, the 1930 jeweled watch reflects the creative partnership between Puissant and René Sim-Lacaze.

Puissant took charge of the studios after her husband's untimely death, and with Sim-Lacaze's support, she designed geometric ladies watches that were prized as the ultimate in elegance at the time.

squares in Paris, Van Cleef & Arpels pays tribute with this range of watches.

Home to Van Cleef & Arpels since 1906, Place Vendôme is a natural source of inspiration. In perfect symmetry with the pure lines of the identical townhouses surrounding the square, the Façade watches reveal the brilliant modernity of a classical design through its arches and design work illustrating masonry.

Water-resistant to 30 meters, Façade is available in unisex or mini-ladies sizes in 18K yellow or white gold, steel or yellow gold and steel. The spare, white lacquered dial elegantly houses four Roman numerals, the minute and hour hand, and the Van Cleef & Arpels signature. Arching upward of the XII, the dial is surrounded by a keystone detail and two barlugs fasten the rectangular case to a brickwork gold band or leather bands. Diamonds and rubies adorn the barlugs and keystone in the jeweled versions.

Each timepiece reveals the beauty of Paris — its undisputed status as the world capital of architecture and luxury goods — as well as the famous facade of Van Cleef & Arpels, well-known to the watchmaker's loyal and adoring clients as "22 Place Vendôme."

Round, square and cylindrical watch faces boast gemstones — either a sapphire, ruby or emerald — circled by diamonds, in white or yellow gold, these watches are gracefully paired with satin straps in bright or pale colors reflective of this famous era.

Façade Watches

Van Cleef & Arpels' Façade watch traces its roots to the end of Louis XIV's reign, when Jules Hardouin-Mansart designed the elegant Place Vendôme. Rich in history and renowned as one of the most beautiful of the five Royal

Top left: "Façade" watch. Case in 18K yellow gold with ruby trapezium (0.19 carats) at 12 o'clock, attachment at 6 o'clock set with seven rubies (0.69 carats) and attachment at 12 o'clock set with 22 diamonds (0.23 carats). Bracelet in 18K yellow gold.

Left: "Façade" watch. Case in 18K yellow gold with emerald trapezium at 12 o'clock (0.14 carats), attachment at 6 o'clock set with 25 diamonds (0.27 carats) and attachment at 12 o'clock set with 22 diamonds (0.23 carats). Buckle in 18K yellow gold and strap in green full skin crocodile.

Bibliography

Aveni, Anthony. Empires of Time. New York: Basic Books, Inc.,1989.

Baillie, G. H., C. Clutton, C.A. Ilbert. Britten's Old Clocks and Watches and their Makers. New York: Bonanza Books, 1956.

Barracca, Jader, Giampiero Negretti, Franco Nencini. Le Temps de Cartier. Milan, Wrist International S.r.l., 1989.

Bayer, Patricia. Art Deco Source Book. Secaucus, NJ: Wellfleet Press, 1988.

Bouillon, Jean-Paul. Art Deco. New York: Skira, Rizzoli International Publications, Inc., 1989.

Breguet, Emmanuel. Breguet. Watchmakers Since 1775. Paris: Alain de Gourvuff, editor, 1997.

Brunner, Gisbert, Christian Pfeiffer-Belli, Martin K. Wehrli. Audemars Piguet. Masterpieces of Classical Watchmaking. Audemars Piguet,1993.

Brunner, Gisbert L., Marc Sich. Mastering Time. Paris, France: Editions Assouline, 1997.

Cardinal, Catherine. Watchmaking in History, Art and Science. Scriptar S.A., 1984.

Cipolla, Carlo. Clocks & Culture. New York: Walker & Company, 1967.

Cologni, Franco, Gimapiero Negertti, Franco Nencini. Piaget Watches and Wonders. Abbeville Press Publishers, 1994.

Cologni, Franco, Eric Nussbaum. Platinum by Cartier. Triumphs of the Jewelers' Art. Harry N. Abrams, Inc., Publishers, 1995.

Coveney, Peter, Roger Highfield. The Arrow of Time. New York: Fawcett Columbine, 1990.

Cowan, Harrison. Time and Its Measurement. World Publishing Co., 1958.

Darton, Mike, editor. Art Deco, An Illustrated Guide to the Decorative Style 1920-40. Secaucus, NJ: Wellfleet Press, 1989.

de Carle, Donald. Watch & Clock Encyclopedia. New York: Bonanza Books, 1977.

Fleet, Simon. Clocks. Octopus Books, 1961.

Fritz, Manfred. Reverso. The Living Legend. Jaeger-Le Coultre. Edition Braus, 1992.

Guye, Samuel, Henri Michel. Time & Space. Praeger Publishing, 1971.

Hohren-Van Rossum, Gerhard. History of the Hour. University of Chicago Press, 1992. Huber, Martin, Alan Banberry in collaboration with Gisbert L. Brunner. Patek Philippe Geneve. Antiquorum, 1988.

Humbert, B. The Chronograph; Its Mechanism and Repair. La Conversion (Switzerland) Editions Scriptar S.A., 1990.

Jagger, Cedric. The Artistry of the English Watch. Rutland, VT: Charles E. Tuttle Company,1988.

Jendritzki, H. The Watchmaker and his Lathe. Scriptar S.A.,1982.

Jespersen, James, Jane Fitz-Randolph. From Sundials to Atomic Clocks. U.S. Department of Commerce, 1977.

Lambelet, Carole, Lorette Coen. The World of Vacheron Constantin Geneve. Scriptar SA/Vacheron Constantin Geneve, 1992.

Lang, Gerd-R, Reinhard Meis. Chronograph Wristwatches to Stop Time. Atglen, PA: Schiffer Publishing, Ltd., 1993.

Neal, Harry Edward. The Mystery of Time. New York: Julian Messner, division of Pocket Books, Inc., 1966.

Pippa, Luigi. Masterpieces of Watchmaking. Scriptar S.A. / Sperling & Kupfer Editori S.P.A., 1966.

Richter, Benno. Bretiling. The History of a Great Brand of Watches. Atglen, PA: Schiffer Publishing Ltd., 1995.

Scarisbrick, Diana. Chaumet. Master Jewellers since 1780. Alain de Gourcuff editor, 1995.

Tolke, Hans-F, Jurgen King. IWC, International Watch Co., Schaffhausen. Zurich, Switzerland: Verlag Ineichen,1987.

Uhrenmuseum Beyer Zurich. Antike Uhren. Callwey Verlag Munchen. 1996.

Von Osterhausen, Fritz. The Movado History. Atglen, PA: Schiffer Publishing Ltd., 1996.

Waugh, Albert E. Sundials: Their Theory & Construction. New York: Publishers Inc., 1973.

Welch, Kenneth F. The History of Clocks & Watches. Drake Publishers, Inc., 1972.

Williams, Brian and Brend. The Random House book of 1001 Wonders of Science. New York: Random House, Inc., 1989.

Photo Credits

p.14: Beyer Museum/Zurich. p.15: Beyer Museum/Zurich. p.16: Roberta Naas. p.17: Beyer Museum/Zurich, Roberta Naas. p.18: Beyer Museum/Zurich, Roberta Naas. p.19: Beyer Museum/Zurich. p.20: Beyer/Zurich, Scriptar S.A., background courtesy Beyer/Zurich. p.21: Beyer/Zurich, Scriptar, S.A. p.22: Scriptar S.A., IWC (International Watch Co.), background courtesy of IWC. p.23: Scriptar S.A.

p.24: Vacheron Constantin. p.25: Vacheron Constantin. p.26: Beyer/Zurich, Scriptar S.A., Vacheron Constantin. p.27: Beyer/Zurich, Antiquorum, Vacheron Constantin. p.28: Breguet, Beyer/Zurich, background courtesy Swiss Tourism Bureau. p.29: Patek Philippe, Perrelet, Chopard. p.30: Girard-Perregaux, Scriptar S.A., background courtesy Vacheron Constantin. p.31: Chopard, Omega, Vacheron Constantin. p.32: Cartier, Jaeger-LeCoultre. p.33: Antiquorum, Breitling, IWC. p.34: Audemars Piguet, Franck Muller, Hamilton, Rolex. p.35: Breitling, Concord, Jaeger-LeCoultre, Omega, background courtesy Omega/NASA.

p.36: Breguet. p.37: Breguet. p.38: Blancpain, Robergé, Omega, background courtesy Blancpain. p.39: Girard-Perregaux, Chopard. p.40: Franck Muller, Daniel Roth. p.41: Chopard, Patek Philippe. p.42: Cartier, Breguet, Vacheron Constantin, background courtesy Audemars Piguet. p.43: IWC. p.44: Jaeger-LeCoultre, Audemars Piguet, Patek Philippe. p.45: Piaget, Jaeger-LeCoultre. p.46: Jaeger-LeCoultre, Robergé, Piaget. p.47: Franck Muller, Concord, background courtesy Jaeger-LeCoultre. p.48: Jaeger-LeCoultre, Concord, Blancpain. p.49: Breguet, Vacheron Constantin, Audemars Piguet.

p.50: Breitling. p.51: Breitling. p.52: Breguet, Chopard, Omega, Blancpain, background courtesy Longines. p.53: Franck Muller, Baume & Mercier. p.54: Breitling, Girard-Perregaux, background courtesy Breitling. p.55: Omega, Philippe Charriol, Robergé. p.56: Rolex, Blancpain, TAG-Heuer, Hublot, background courtesy Vacheron Constantin. p.57: Chaumet, Longines, Vacheron Constantin, Robergé. p.58: Harry Winston, Breitling, Patek Philippe. p.59: Gianni Versace, Chopard, Vacheron Constantin, Robergé.

p.60: Van Cleef & Arpels. p.61: Van Cleef & Arpels. p.62: Chaumet. p. 63: Cartier, Chaumet, Vacheron Constantin. p.64: Vacheron Constantin. p.65: Patek Philippe, Girard-Perregaux, Concord, background and art courtesy Chaumet. p.66: Baume & Mercier. p.67: Omega, Movado, Van Cleef & Arpels, background courtesy Breitling.

p.68: Piaget. p.69: Piaget. p.70: Chopard, Breguet, background courtesy Audemars Piguet. p.71: Harry Winston, Chaumet, Concord. p.72: Patek Philippe, Vacheron Constantin, Chopard, background courtesy Patek Philippe. p.73: Audemars Piguet, Bertolucci, Breguet, Concord. p.74: Robergé, Bulgari, Corum. p.75: Van Cleef & Arpels, Chopard. p.76: Cartier, Van Cleef & Arpels, Harry Winston, background courtesy Breguet. p.77: Concord, Girard-Perregaux, Rolex, Omega.

p.78: Jaeger-LeCoultre. p.79: Jaeger-LeCoultre. p.80: Scriptar, S.A. p.81: Girard-Perregaux, IWC, Chaumet. p.82: Van Cleef & Arpels, Piaget. p.83: Vacheron Constantin, Chanel, Universal Geneve, Chronoswiss, Ebel. p.84: Cartier, Omega, Corum. p.85: Piaget, Van Cleef & Arpels, Bulgari.

p.86: Patek Philippe. p.87: Patek Philippe. p.88: Chaumet, Cartier, Patek Philippe, Breguet. p.89: Jaeger-LeCoultre, Harry Winston, Cartier, IWC, Piaget. p.90: Chopard, Breitling, Omega, Concord. p.91: Jaeger-LeCoultre, Cartier, Franck Muller, Omega, Cartier.

p.92-97: Blancpain. p.98-105: Breguet. p.106-111: Breitling. p.112-117: Chaumet. p.118-125: Chopard. p.126-131: Concord. p.132-139: Franck Muller. p.140-145: Girard-Perregaux. p.146-151: Harry Winston. p.152-159: Jaeger-LeCoultre. p.160-167: Omega. p.168-177: Patek Philippe. p.178-185: Piaget. p.186-193: Robergé. p.194-201: Vacheron Constantin. p.202-207: Van Cleef & Arpels.